SHAKESPEARE HERMENEUTICS,
or
THE STILL LION.

SHAKESPEARE HERMENEUTICS,

or

The Still Lion,

Being an Essay towards the Restoration of Shakespeare's
Text.

BY

C. M. INGLEBY, M.A., LL.D.,

OF TRINITY COLLEGE, CAMBRIDGE.

HASKELL HOUSE PUBLISHERS LTD.
Publishers of Scarce Scholarly Books
NEW YORK. N. Y. 10012
1971

First Published 1875

822.33
DI5|s

HASKELL HOUSE PUBLISHERS Ltd.
Publishers of Scarce Scholarly Books
280 LAFAYETTE STREET
NEW YORK. N. Y. 10012

Library of Congress Catalog Card Number: 73–157552

Standard Book Number 8383-1294-2

Printed in the United States of America
78-7580

Note.

THE ensuing essay was originally written for the *Jahrbücher* of the German Shakespeare Society, and was published at Berlin in the volume for 1867. The author saw but one proof of it before its publication, and in consequence the imprint was disfigured by an immense number of press-errors, only a few of which were detected before the volume was issued.

The editor, Dr. Friedrich von Bodenstedt, voluntarily conceded to the author of the essay the Society's permission to reprint it in England. This, however, was not done till 1874-5, when, owing to the pressure put upon him by several of his friends—in particular by Mr. Joseph Crosby, of Zanesville, Ohio, and Mr. C. J. Monro, of Hadley—the author enlarged and reprinted it, and presented the edition to the New Shakspere Society.

As there was still an unsatisfied demand for the little volume, he has once more enlarged and reprinted it; and it is now, for the first time, published in England.

Table of Contents.

—*0*—

ERRATA.

———

PAGE	LINE	
35	1	dele 'Vertomannus.'
35	20	prefix 'In' to 'Norfolk.'
38	4	for 'Phillips' read 'Phillipps.'
73	16	„ 'three fingers' „ 'forefinger.'
74	24	prefix 'vol. v' to 'p. 581.'
95	antepenult.	for '1' read '2.'
95	penult.	„ 'Venus' „ 'Adonis.'
106	27	„ 'G. W.' „ 'W. G.'
107	25	add '& 26' to 'April 12.'
107	25	„ '& 3' to 'Jan. 31.'
113	15	prefix 'the *ductus literarum*,' to 'the leading.'
119	6	for '72' read '68.'
121	3	„ 'the' „ 'their.' *
133	18	„ 'bacchanial' „ 'bacchanalian.'
137	3	„ 'Hamlet's' „ 'Bernardo's.'
156	2	„ '2' „ '1'
167	add 'Maundevile, Sir J. . . . . 41.'	

* An example of the class of misprints mentioned and illustrated on pp. 118, 119.

THE STILL LION.

THE STILL LION DISCOVERED.

WE may say of Shakespeare's text what Thomas De Quincey said of Milton's :

' ON ANY ATTEMPT TO TAKE LIBERTIES WITH A PASSAGE OF *HIS*, YOU FEEL AS WHEN COMING, IN A FOREST, UPON WHAT SEEMS A DEAD LION ; PERHAPS HE MAY *NOT* BE DEAD, BUT ONLY SLEEPING, NAY PERHAPS HE MAY NOT BE SLEEPING, BUT ONLY SHAMMING. * * * * You may be put down with shame by some man reading the line otherwise,'

or, we add, reading it in the light of more extended or more accurate knowledge.

Here lies the covert danger of emendation. It is true that the text of Shakespeare, as it comes down to us—" the latest seed of time "—in the folio 1623, as well as in the early quartos, is very corrupt. It is corrupt on two accounts. As to the text of the quartos, there was no proper editorial super-vision, since the editions were intended merely for the accom-modation of play-goers ; the text was therefore imperfect not only in form but in substance as well. As to the text of the folio, the supervision of Messrs. Heminge and Condell seems to have been confined to the selection of copies for the printers, Messrs. Jaggard and Blount; and some of those were play-house copies, which had been curtalled for representation, and certain other were copies of quarto editions; while the correction of the press was probably left to the 'reader' of the printing-house,* who certainly could not have exercised any extraordinary vigilance in his vocation. Accordingly we have imperfect copies at first, and a misprinted text at last.

The corrupt and mutilated condition in which the Greek and Roman Classics, especially the Greek, have been handed down to modern times is the sufficient reason for that latitude of conjectural criticism which has been brought to bear on their ancient texts. If we had to deal with an English text which bore like evidences of dilapidation, we should naturally have recourse to the same means for its correction. But such is not the case with the works of any English author who has assumed the proportions of a classic: not Chaucer, nor Shakespeare, nor Milton, is a venerable ruin demanding restoration; though Shakespeare, far more than Milton, has suffered corruption, and that by the very nature of the vehicle to which he committed his thoughts; exactly as the 'Last Supper' of Leonardo da Vinci has incurred an amount of destruction which it might have escaped had it been painted on wood or on canvass. Such corruption, however, as infects the works of Shakespeare touches but comparatively small, and often isolated, portions of the text, offering no very serious obstacle to the general reader,

---

* Not improbably Edward Blount, Isaac Jaggard's partner. See *Notes and Queries*, 2nd S. iii. 7.

who is not exacting or scrupulous in the interpretation of his author's phraseology. Patches of indictable nonsense, which have hitherto defied all attempts at elucidation, there are, as we shall soon see, in some of the plays; yet it is no very violent proceeding to regard them as parts of the inferior work of a joint-author, or as interpolations by the players, or as matter adopted by Shakespeare from the older play on which his own was founded. But the critical student is naturally intolerant of every unexplored obscurity and every unresolved difficulty; and an editor who works for students as well as for general readers feels himself bound to apply to the text all the available resources of criticism. The example of the ancient Classics, and the capital success which rewarded the vigilance and invention of scholars in that field, could not fail to determine the method on which the recension of Shakespeare was to be attempted by the verbal critics.

As the natural result, the text has been subjected to a conjectural criticism which owns no restraint and systematically violates every principle of probability and of propriety. Obsolete phraseology and archaic allusion are treated as cases of corruption: the language, where corrupt, instead of being restored or amended, is modernized and *improved:* and the idiom, instead of being expounded and illustrated, is accommodated to the prevailing grammatical standard. By this means more fatuous and incapable nonsense has been manufactured for Shakespeare than can be found in any of the ancient copies of his plays.

The text of Milton, on the other hand, offers little or no

holding for the conjectural critic.*   One might have predicted
that of all English texts it was the least likely to have afforded
congenial sport to a classical scholar intent on havoc.   But it
was not so much the promise of the coverts, but the solicitations
of exalted rank, that induced the combative and tenacious old
Master of Trinity, when he had already earned his laurels as an
editor of the Classics, and 'won his spurs' as a verbal critic of
matchless resource and felicity, even in the 69th year of his
age, to undertake the recension of *Paradise Lost.*   As some
sort of self-justification he framed the hypothesis that Milton's
text had suffered through the carelessness and also the invention of the scribe to whom it had been dictated by the blind
bard.   Bentley was a great man, and this work of his is great
in its way.   He mars his author with power and splendour,

* The *systematic* departure from the ordinary spelling of the time in
the text of the *Paradise Lost* of 1667 has been noticed by De Quincey.
Mr. B. M. Pickering says :
'At the end of the first edition of *Paradise Lost* we meet with what, to
a casual observer, would appear to be a very singular correction, *viz.* Lib.
2. v. 414, "For *we* read wee."   Even a tolerably attentive student of the
early editions of Milton might be at a loss what to make of this.   It is
certain that *we* is to be met with in this edition of *Paradise Lost* quite as
often, or rather oftener, with a single than with a double *e.*   It occurs as *we*
in the very next line to that referred to in this errata.   The explanation is
this :—that although in ordinary cases Milton is accustomed to spell the
pronouns *we*, *me*, *he*, *ye*, with a single *e*, whenever special emphasis is intended to be put upon them he makes a point of writing *wee*, *mee*, *hee*, *yee*.
Many other words are differently spelt to what was then, or is now, usual,
and this not in an uncertain manner, as is common in old books, but after a
regular, unvarying system, deliberately formed by Milton himself, and
adopted upon choice and afore-thought.' (From the Prospectus of A
Reprint of the First Edition of *Paradise Lost.*)

and we admire his learning and talents, while we deplore their misapplication.

This reference to Milton, WHO IS ALSO A STILL LION, THRILLING INDEED WITH LIFE, BUT OFTEN DISSEMBLING HIS VITALITY, leads me to exhibit the salient contrasts between the two English classics of the seventeenth century. I will first consider the works themselves as intellectual achievements : secondly, the material vehicle of their transmission.

(1) Dramatic Literature, out of the very reason for its existence, is more within the compass of the ordinary understanding than an epic poem. Its appeal is to the common mind. If the people fail to catch the meaning of a dialogue or a soliloquy, it is a mere impertinence, how splendid soever may be its diction, or profound the reach of its thought. Shakespeare is, indeed, very strongly differenced from his contemporaries by the fervour of his imagination and his knowledge of human nature, as well as by the strength and range of his vocabulary ; and certain portions of his works are pitched in as sublime a key as the epics of Milton. But on the whole the language of Shakespeare is more or less amenable to undisciplined good sense. Milton, on the contrary, 'flies an eagle's flight,' and is quite out of the blank of the general aim. He is 'caviary to the general,' and, without the poetic temperament, the strongest common sense and the most delicate ear for rhythm are quite at fault in the criticism of his greater works.

With this distinction in mind, the reason of Bentley's deplorable failure in attempting an edition of *Paradise Lost* is not far to seek. The work he had successfully done was in the field of the Greek and Latin Classics, the emendation of which, as that of our early dramatic literature, is generally within the range of that strong natural sense for which Bentley was so conspicuous : and this, complemented with his matchless ingenuity and vast book-learning, was amply sufficient for his purpose.* One almost wonders that he did not make the experiment on Shakespeare rather than on Milton ; and it seems natural to fancy that, had he known in what relationship of marriage he stood to the Bard of Avon,† he would have been drawn to the recension of his great relative's works, and would have brought to the task that reverential affection which is so conspicuously absent from his notes on Milton.

(2) The difference in the 'material vehicle' consists in the difference between Dramatic Art and Literature. We must consider this point at somewhat greater length than the former. Disallowing Bentley's pretext, as a mere device for the indulgence of licentious criticism, which especially in the case of Milton *sufflaminandus est*, it is plain that Milton's epics enjoyed the benefit of being printed, if not under the eye, at least under the direct superintendence, of their author ; and we know, moreover, that in exercising that function he was fastidiously vigilant and accurate. We may be quite sure that the text contains but very few misprints, and that conjecture has no *locus standi* there. But how different was the case with

---

* See De Quincey's articles on *Bentley* and *Landor*.
† The relationship is easily stated, though it is very remote. Shakespeare's granddaughter married (secondly) the brother of Mrs. Bentley's grandfather.

the dramas of Shakespeare ! Speaking of the textual vehicle
only, we may be equally sure that the conjectural critic would
have had 'the very cipher of a function' if those works had
received the final corrections and editorial supervision of their
author. They would still have been thronged with difficulties,
and pestered with obscurities, taxing the utmost erudition and
study of the editor, the greater number of which would have
belonged to the class *historical*, consisting wholly of allusions
to forgotten persons and events, and to obsolete habits and
customs. Not a few, however, of those difficulties would have
belonged to the class *grammatical*, demanding on the part of
the expositor almost as much learning and research as the
historical allusions in the text : for since the date of Shakespeare's *floruit* the English language has suffered no incon-
siderable change, though much less than the habits and
customs of the English people.

But Shakespeare died without, so far as we know, having
made the attempt to collect and print his works. Of this fact
an unnecessary difficulty has been made. A much more self-
conscious genius than Shakespeare has himself given us the
clue to its solution, a clue of which all writers, save Thomas
Carlyle,* have failed to perceive the significance. Goethe con-
fessed to Eckermann that he never reperused any of his poems
when once it was completed and printed, unless impelled to
the task by the demand for a new edition ; and that he then
read it with no self-complacency, but rather dissatisfaction.
Why was this ? Simply because he felt a *Widerwille*, or

* Consult his *Shooting Niagara, and after?*

distaste, towards the offspring of his less matured self, by
reason of its inadequacy to express his great ideal—the 'un-
bodied figure of the thought that gave 't surmised shape.'
He had outgrown his own powers, in the grander sense of
that phrase : never, like poor Swift, living to look back with
wonder and horror on the glory of a genius that he owned
no more, but prejudicially contrasting his past self with the
greater present.

'As for what I have done,' he would repeatedly say to me, 'I take
no pride in it whatever. Excellent poets have lived at the same time with
myself, poets more excellent have lived before me, and others will come
after me.' (*Gespräche mit Goethe*, 1836, vol. i. p. 86. Feb. 19th, 1829.
Oxenford's Translation, 1850, vol. ii. p. 145.)

He also says to Falk ("with unusual rapidity and vehe-
mence") :

"I will not hear anything of the matter ; neither of the public, nor
of posterity, nor of the justice, as you call it, which is hereafter to reward
my efforts. I hate my *Tasso*, just because people say that it will go down
to posterity; I hate *Iphigenie ;* in a word, I hate everything of mine that
pleases the public. I know that it belongs to the day, and the day to it ;
but I tell you, once for all, I will not live for the day." *Characteristics
of Goethe*, by Sarah Austin, 1873, vol. i. p. 112.

He had, seemingly, that very contempt for self-complacency
which he attributes to Faust—

'Verflucht voraus die hohe Meinung,
   Womit der Geist sich selbst umfängt.'

Now Shakespeare wrote and issued under his own eye two
poems as literature, and nothing else. The rest of his works,
save his sonnets and minor pieces, were written for represent-

ation on the boards, and as a simple matter of money-profit. Not faultless even as dramas, they must have fully answered his primary aim, which was mercenary, but not that grand ideal which dwelt 'deep down in his heart of hearts.' Hence he must have viewed them with some dissatisfaction, (1) as not being in the best sense Literature; (2) as being 'mere implorators of—mercenary, if not—unholy suits,' designed to catch the penny with the least pains; (3) as being often hasty and inchoate, and always imperfect, attempts to realize his own ideal. From the effort of recasting and revising them he naturally shrank. If he gave a thought to the probability of his works becoming his country's crowning glory, it might very reasonably have occurred to him that no revision would be likely to guarantee them an exemption from the common lot which was not the due of their original merits. Of one thing we may be quite sure, that Shakespeare's good sense and honesty of purpose rendered him perfectly indifferent to that vanity of vanities which Goethe, in the speech from which a citation has already been made, calls 'das Blenden der Erscheinung,' for which so many a man of letters has sacrificed the calm and comfort of his life.

Be all that as it may, it is a fact that the first collection of his plays was published six or seven years after his death; and it is a matter of certainty that the folio of 1623 was printed from inaccurate quarto editions and mutilated stage-copies. This is the 'case' of those who advocate the rights of unlimited conjecture; and we frankly make the concession, that our text needs emendation. But, before they can be

permitted to conjecture, we require of them to find out where
the corruptions lie. If a man's body be diseased, the seat of
the disease can generally be determined, between the patient
and the doctor: in some cases, however, the malady baffles
alike research and experiment.

In the case of Shakespeare's text, the diagnosis is infinitely
perplexed: (1) from the multitude of obscurities and difficulties
that beset it: (2) from the close resemblance that often sub-
sists between those obscurities which spring from the obsolete
language or the archaic allusions, and those which are wholly
due to the misreading or misprinting of the text. Our healthy
parts are so like our diseased parts, that the doctor sets about
the medicinal treatment of that which needs no cure ; and
the patient's body is so full of those seeming anomalies, that
his life is endangered by the multiplicity of agencies brought
to bear on his time-worn frame.

What, if there are cases in which those κύριοι συνωμόται,
archaic phraseology and textual corruption, unite their powers
against us ? Why, in such cases, it is most likely that the
critic would be utterly baffled : that he would be unable to
restore the lost integrity even by the combined forces of
exposition and conjecture. Now it so happens that after all
that contemporary literature and conjectural criticism could
do for Shakespeare's immortal works, there is a residue of
about thirty-five to forty passages which have defied all
attempts to cure their immortal nonsense. Does it not seem
likely that the perplexity in such cases is due to the joint
action of those two sources of obscurity, and our inability to

persever or discriminate the one from the other? We shall see. The *vintage* afforded by these remarks may be thus expressed. Conjectural criticism is legitimate; for it is needful to the perfection of the text: but no critic can be licensed to exercise it whose knowledge and culture do not guarantee these three great pre-requisites: (1) a competent knowledge of the orthography, phraseology, prosody, as well as the language of arts and customs, prevalent in the time of Shakespeare: (2) a delicate ear for the rhythm of verse and prose:* (3) a reverential faith in the resources of Shakespeare's genius.

The present time seems most fitting for the treatment of the question: To what extent, and in what manner, may conjectural criticism be safely exercised? For the last twenty years the text of Shakespeare has been subjected to a process, which for its wholesale destructiveness and the arrogance of its pretensions is wholly without parallel. The English press has teemed with works, from Mr. J. P. Collier's pseudo-antique Corrector down to the late Mr. Staunton's papers 'On Unsuspected Corruptions in the Text of Shakespeare,' most of which, in our judgment, have achieved no other result than that of corrupting and beraying the ancient text. We allow that some of the conjectures thus put forth are invaluable, and certain other may be entertained for careful consideration ; but the mass we repudiate as impertinent and barbarous. We

---

* The late Mr. Staunton was deficient in this. Such a symptosis as would be introduced into the text by reading, in *Macbeth*, 'Making the *green zone* red' and '*cleanse* the *clogg'd* bosom,' &c., would (to borrow De Quincey's happy phrase) 'splinter the teeth of a crocodile,' and make the adder shake her ears.

deny the need of any wholesale change, and impute great ignorance to the assailants :—not to insist on matters of taste, which it is proverbially difficult to make matters of controversy. We are fully able to prove the strength of our position, by showing that the passages attacked are proof against innovation by the power of their own sense. To do this at full length and in complete detail would require the dimensions of a large volume : to teach the general truth by the force of particular examples is all that we now propose to accomplish. This is our aim : to exemplify the growth of the written English language in relation to the text of Shakespeare : to point out the dangers incident to all tampering with special words and phrases in it : to examine and defend certain of its words and phrases which have suffered the wrongs of so-called emendation ; and finally to discuss the general subject of the emendation of the text, and to adduce some examples of passages reclaimed or restored through this means. Having accomplished this, we shall gladly leave the old text, with its legion of archaisms and corruptions, to the tender mercies of those critics whose object is to conserve what is sound and to restore what is corrupt, and not at all to improve what, to their imperfect judgment and limited knowledge, seems unsatisfactory. To the arbitration of such critics we submit the question, whether in any particular case a word or phrase which is intelligible to the well-informed reader, however strange or uncouth, does or does not fulfil the utmost requirements of the cultivated mind, regard being had to the context, the situation, and the speaker.

CHAPTER I.

ON THE GROWTH OF THE ENGLISH LANGUAGE IN RELATION TO THE TEXT OF SHAKESPEARE.

GREAT is the mystery of archaic spelling. Let us consider a few caprices of spelling, before proceeding to notice the vitality and consequent instability of written words : just as we must consider the symbolizing and uses of words before the grammatical structure and force of phrases. The word (ῥῆμα), rightly regarded, is an expressed *ens rationis*. It is purely a matter of convenience, whether it shall be represented to the eye or to the ear. We hold those to be in the wrong who would wholly subordinate the written sign to the sound, as if writing were *de jure*, as it is *de facto*, a secondary process ; and herein we dissent from the teaching of thorough-going Phoneticians. Be that as it may, the object of writing and speaking is not to *impart* the inner word (νόημα) : for transmission of aught from one man's mind to another is impossible : but to *suggest* it. Still, in effect, something is communicated, or made common, to both minds. In order that we may suggest to another man's mind any word that is in our own, we employ a medium which will stand for it, and lead him to understand it as we do. The written word is simply such a mediatorial symbol. The letters which constitute it are used to represent vocal sounds; and these may be of very variable force and range, while the word so symbolized is invariable. Thus *ea* and *a*, or *ea* and *e*, may by agreement represent the same vowel-sound; and *j* and *g*, or *j* and *i*, may, according to circumstances, stand for the same consonant-sound. But, further, several written symbols that have little or nothing in common may stand for the same inner word : much more may two written symbols, which have grown by habit and custom from one spoken symbol, be regarded as equivalent forms of, or rather terms for, one and the same word. Thus, in the relative literature we have *purture* and *pourtray*, *scase* and *scarce*, *scorce* and *scar*, *moe* and *more*, *windoe* and *windore*, *kele* and *cool*, *kill* and *quell*, *leese* and *lose*, *meve* and *move*, *cusse* and *kiss*, *make* and *mate*, &c. Not a shade of difference exists between the words in any of these pairs, unless, perhaps, in *scorce* and *scar*, the latter—and possibly not the former—having sometimes the sense of *value*, while both mean *barter*. Conversely several written symbols, which in the letter are identical, may not only stand for as many distinct words, but may be themselves also radically distinct. We have *must* (new wine), *must* (stale smell or taste), and *must* (il faut); *mere* (mare), *mere* (lake), and *mere* (pure); *sound* (sonus), *sound* (sanus, whole), *sound* (arm of the sea), a word possibly related to *swim*, or otherwise to *sunder; sound* (the swimming-bladder of the codfish), *sound* (sonder, to fathom), *sound* (swoon). These two classes of word-couples are not to be confounded with words which have only the same sound, without either similarity of sense or identity of spelling : e. g., *ought, aught, ort :* nor yet with those which have only the same spelling, without either similarity of sense or identity of sound : e. g., *lead* or *tear.* The main points to keep distinctly in view in this study, are that the orthography of the written symbol, like its vocal expression, may change to almost any extent, and yet the internal word signified by such letters or sounds may remain unaltered ; and that the written or spoken symbol may remain unchanged, while the word signified changes, or that symbol may be used for words which have not a common origin.

Shakespeare has had many ugly charges brought against him. Among others he has been arraigned for bad spelling and bad grammar ! But what Shakespeare's orthography was we have no certain means of knowing. If he had any system of spelling he was a century in advance of his contemporaries. We have no knowledge beyond the capricious orthography of the compositors who set up his works. At the present day words are spelt according to a standard that is subject to only very slight variations. But even as late as the Commonwealth it may be truly affirmed that there was nothing like a standard. In the reigns of Elizabeth and James there was no attempt to ensure uniformity of spelling, nor is it likely that the writers or the readers of that time were conscious of any need or want

---

* Mr. A. J. Ellis and Mr. A. M. Bell hear a glide in this word which we do not. There is a glide in *fort* and *port*, but we do not detect it in *ort* or *sort*. Of course, if the r be sounded as in French, *ort* is at once differentiated from *ought* and *aught*.

in that respect. The question, what determined the orthography
of the time, is exceedingly puzzling. We can here only record
our growing conviction that silent reading was then much
more than at present a purely mental process, and that the
handwriters and printers of that day presented their readers
with nothing incongruous or absurd when they indulged in
the most outrageous versatility of literal construction. That
i and *j*, or *u* and *v*,* should have been regarded as identical
consonants, or that *u* and *w*, or *i* and *y*, should have been
regarded as identical vowels (though the least extraordinary
of the many anomalies of their spelling), is quite enough to
prove that readers were not fastidious on such points. One is
sometimes disposed to wonder whether particular provinces
had not, somewhat earlier, their conventional forms of spelling
peculiarly adapted to the pronunciation prevalent in each pro-
vince, which became at length confusedly intermingled through
the practice of engaging handwriters and compositors of various
provinces to do the work of one establishment. There were,
indeed, in Shakespeare's day, limits to their vagaries. So far
as we have been able to settle the point, few words were
allowed as many as a dozen different forms of spelling. The
word which we write *swoon* (a fainting-fit, or to faint) is a

---

* The Rev. F. G. Fleay, in the *Athenæum*, September 26, 1874, pretends
to discover a difference between the same word spelt under the *v* and under
the *u* orthography. 'Thus we have *recover*, *recouer*, and *recure* side by side;
divell and *deule; even, euen*, and *eene; live, liue*, and *lie;* and many others.
The last of these is especially important, and explains several difficulties in
Shakspere.' We record this as a 'curiosity of Shakespeare criticism.' We
suppose Mr. Fleay, in *Coriolanus* iv. 7, 50 (Globe Ed.) sees *live* in *lie.*

very curious example of Protean versatility. In a *Nominale* of the fifteenth century, edited by Mr. Thomas Wright, F.S.A., the word is figured *swoyne.* Chaucer and Lord Bacon have it, *swoun* or *swoune.* In the State Trials, 1338, it is *swoon;* and so we find it in Milton, Dryden, and all the moderns. But Fabyan, 1364, spells it *swown* or *swowne,* and Spenser, 1589, and Walkington, 1607, adopt the same orthography; North, Shakespeare, and sundry other authors give it *sound;* and in Richard Hyrde's translations it is generally *swone!*

Within an assignable limit for each word, we may rest assured that every compositor in a printing-house spelt pretty much as seemed good in his own eyes. That he had just set up a word in one literal form was, perhaps, a reason why he should, on its recurrence, spell it in some other way. The spelling of all words, in fact, like that of Sam Weller's surname, depended ' upon the taste and fancy of the writer ' or of the printer; and just as pedants with us will sacrifice the exact render of their best thoughts in order to avoid the repetition of a word (of all pedantries the most contemptible and reprehensible), so did an Elizabethan compositor sacrifice a just and compendious form of spelling to his love of variety and his contempt of uniformity. If he had set up *foorth, poore, woorse,* he would on the next occasion present these words in the more concise style, *forth, pore, worse.* If he had set up *brydde* for the feathered biped, that feat of ' composition ' became, if anything, a reason for transposing the *r* and *y;* for omitting a *d,* or the final vowel, or both; or for substituting *i* for *y,* on the next occasion when he had to cope with that Protean customer.

D

To have printed, 'Among the bryddes the blackbrydde hath the saddest coat, and the moaste dulceate mellodie,' would have been an offence against the established economy, which dictated as much prodigality as was consistent with convenience; for apart from custom, which always has more weight than it deserves, the probability is that the compositor could not have conformed to a standard of orthography (if such a thing had ever occurred to him as desirable on other grounds) without constant embarrassment and frequent unsightliness in the make-up of his lines.   Obviously, poetical works, in which the lines do not run on and may always be adjusted without dividing the final words, did not impose on him the same limitations as prose works.   But even in the latter it does not always appear that the caprices of spelling were due to the necessities of the case; as in the two following examples, taken from Hyrde's translation of Vives' *Instruction of a Christian Woman* (ed. 1592; sig. D 4): the sense is unimportant here:

> and specially if there bee any long
> space betweene the hollydaies. For think
> not y^t holy daies be ordained of the church
> to play on,

Here it is plain that in the second line it would have made no difference to the compositor had he set up 'holy daies' as in the third line; or in the third line 'hollydaies' as in the second line.   Here there was no such necessity as, in a line a little higher on the page, occasioned the composite form 'workingdaies,' instead of 'working daies," which we find in an intermediate line where there was room for the *lead* or the *hyphen.* Indeed it is hard to imagine any reason for omitting the *l* in the second 'holy' which did not equally apply to the first, unless, indeed, the translator intended to exhibit obtrusively the original sense of the compound word, as *sanctæ dies.* In a word, variety in spelling was not always due to the condition of making up the lines without unsightly breaks, but is, at least sometimes, referable to chance or to preference. Again, sig. G 4,

> Let her bee content with a maide not
> faire and wanton,   fayre,

Here 'fayre' is the catch-word at the bottom of one page, and 'faire' is the first word on the next page. So likewise in Edward Phillips' *Theatrum Poetarum,* 1675 (The Modern Poets, p. 34-5), we have

> being for great Invention and Poetic
> heighth   height

where 'height' is the catch-word at the bottom of one page, and 'heighth' the first word on the next page. Again in *The Two Angrie Women of Abington,* Mistress Barnes says,

> 'I am abusde, my sonne, by Goursey's wife.'

On which Philip exclaims,

> 'By Mistresse Goursie!'

How are we to account for the change of orthography in the second example from Vives, unless we suppose that the *y* was thought as good an *i* as *i* itself? How, in the other examples, for the omission of the *h* from the catch-word, and the change of *ey* into *ie,* unless the orthography was thought a matter of

little, or at least of secondary, importance ?   That it was so is
proved by the fact that *y* was commonly used for *i* in manuscript : *e. g.,* in a letter from Sir Walter Cope to Viscount
Cranborne, dated 1604, preserved at Hatfield House, Herts,
we read : ' I have sent and bene all thys morning huntyng for
players Juglers & Such kinde of Creaturs but *fynde* them harde
to *finde,*' &c.   Similarly, I doubt not *ll* was thought no worse
than *l*, and *l* as good as *ll* in such a word as *holyday*, where the
o was not made long as in *holy :* the ear being then, in most
cases, the arbiter of spelling.

In fairness it must be allowed that in some few printed
books of the Elizabethan era some approach to uniformity of
spelling is occasionally discernible ; but there was nothing like
a standard of spelling till nearly a century later.   In the work
from which we took the first two examples (book i. chapter 3),
in the course of a single page *wool* is spelled *woll* and *wooll ;*
in the next page, *woolle ;* in the next, *wolle :* but *wool* is only
found in compounds ; and *woole* not at all !

In order to bring these remarks to a focus, in applying
them to Shakespeare's text, let us confine ourselves to words
of one initial letter, say H.   In Lupton's *Too Good to be True,*
1580, *hair* is spelled twice *haire*, and once *heare*.   It is also
spelled *heare* in Kyngesmyll's *Comforts in Afflictions,* 1585.
The latter is the less usual form.   It occurs, however, in earlier
books than those.   It is used, for instance, in Drant's translation of *Horace's Satyres*, 1566 ; where we read, ' I have shaved
of his *heare :*' as to which passage it must be noted that *of* and
off (like *to* and *too, on* and *one, the* and *thee*) are not always

distinguishable in this literature, save by means of the context.
Accordingly the participial adjective *haired*, being written and
printed *heared, hear'd*, and *heard*, is sometimes presented in a
form identical with the past participle of *hear* (audire).   Here
is an example from Shakespeare's *King John*, v. 2 :

> This un-heard sawcinesse and boyish Troopes,
> The king doth smile at.

where ' un-heard sawcinesse ' is the sauciness of those striplings
whose faces are hairless, and ' whose chins are not yet fledg'd '
(2 *Hen. IV.*, i. 2).   Theobald, who must have been ignorant of
the fact that *unheard* was merely *unhair'd* under an earlier
orthography, proposed *unhair'd* as an emendation.   This is
merely an example of those orthographies, so fertile in confusion and mistake, which coincide where they should diverge,
and diverge where they should coincide.   Wickliff spelt *hard*
(durus) *herd*, both forms being a departure from the A. S. *heard*.
The Elizabethans, who inherited and retained the former style,
spelt *herd* (armentum) *heard;* and *heard* (auditus) *hard;* and
this last they pronounced as we do *hard* (durus); a fashion
which is presupposed in *The Taming of the Shrew*, ii. 1 :

> Well have you *heard*, but something *hard* of hearing !

and in parts of Cambridgeshire and Suffolk we may still hear
the same pronunciation.

  Accordingly, those who would contend that these various
forms of spelling afford evidence of a rude attempt at discrim-
ination and *persevĕrance*, must needs admit that the attempt
was wholly abortive ; for what was gained by distinguishing

heard, hard (auditus) from *heard* (comatus), was lost by confounding it with *hard* (durus) ; and what was gained by distinguishing *hard, heard* (armentum) from *herd* (durus), was lost by confounding it with *heard* (auditus).

Heard (armentum) occurs in *Coriolanus* i. 4, where it has been the occasion of an emendation.

> Enter Martius, cursing.
> All the contagion of the South light on you,
> You shames of Rome: you Heard of Byles and Plagues
> Plaister you ore, that you may be abhorr'd
> Farther than seene, and one infect another
> Against the Winde a mile : you Soules of Geese,
> That beare the shapes of men, &c.

The Johnsonian editors read, after Johnson himself,

> you herd of—Boils and Plagues
> Plaster you o'er, &c.,

making a break after 'of,' as if the violence of Martius' passion left him no time to complete his abusive epithet, through the urgency of the imprecation. From Johnson to Collier every editor understands by *Heard*, armentum, save the latter, who reads 'unheard-of' for 'a herd of:' a conjecture which, like so many other candidates for admission into the text, is good *per se* as a probable misprint, but bad in this place as a substitute for the suspected words. The reason is this. Passion takes concrete forms and avoids generalities. Martius would, in the hands of a master, have been made to denounce a specific malady on the Romans, rather than have weakened the force of his substantives by the prefix 'unheard-of.' But there is yet another reason. We cannot part with *Heard* in the sense of armentum. Twice in this play the people are so designated, and once in *Julius Cæsar:* in all with the same contemptuous usage as in the passage under consideration. We adduce this passage, not because the difficulty admits of removal, but because it does not. It is just one of those which we must be content to take and leave as we find it. A score of suppositions might be made to account for the presence of the preposition 'of.' We might treat that preposition as governing 'boils and plagues,' with the sense of *with;* or, with Johnson, as governed by 'you herd,' followed by an aposiopesis : or we might make 'of' an adverb, equivalent to 'off!' and so forth : all these expedients being about equally unsatisfactory ; and there are still other possibilities to consider. But in such a case it is not decision that is required, but faith. We must stand by the text, and wait.

In a similar manner the male deer was symbolized by *hart* and *hert;* but our *heart* (cor) was generally spelt *hart*, and still earlier *hert,* so that the alternative was no security against confusion.

The passage quoted from *Coriolanus* resembles one in *Timon of Athens,* act iii. last scene :

> Of man and beast the infinite malady
> Crust you quite o'er !

and it might be thought that the latter would be of service in construing or correcting the former. This led our friend Mr. Perkins-Ireland of Knowe-Ware to propose a new expedient for restoring the passage in *Coriolanus;* viz., the supposition that a line is lost! He would read:

> You shames of Rome! you herd of . . . .
> An infinite malady of boils and plagues
> Plaster you o'er, &c.

He argues that the compositor's eye wandered from 'of' in the first line to 'of' in the second, whereby he omitted the first words of that line; and he supposes that the dotted portion was originally furnished with such words as 'timorous deer,' or 'heartless hinds.' All which we must allow to be very ingenious. But to such a method of dealing with a line which is *certainly* corrupt—and the one under consideration is far from being that—there is one serious objection, viz., that the supplied portions rest on no evidence whatever, presenting but one out of a great many equally plausible shifts. If, however, it be argued that such phrases as 'infinite malady,' 'timorous deer,' &c., are more likely to be the missing words, because they are used elsewhere by Shakespeare, it is sufficient to reply, that is a strong argument against them : *e. g.*, forasmuch as 'infinite malady' is used in *Timon of Athens* in a precisely similar passage, it is most improbable that Shakespeare would have employed that phrase in *Coriolanus.* It will be helpful to know that Shakespeare's text cannot be emended in this fashion; for he never repeats himself in repeating the same thought or sentiment.*

* Our friend, seeing this in proof, indignantly disclaims the intention to affirm that the missing words in the second line were, *totidem verbis*, 'an infinite malady;' but he does not tell us what the exact words were. Why augment the mass of indefinite conjectures?

To return from this digression : *help* and *heal* (or *hele*), though two distinct words, must, ages ago, have had a common origin, and are often used by Elizabethan writers indifferently. Thus, in *Phioravante's Secrets*, 1582, the second chapter is headed thus : 'To helpe the Falling Sicknesse in yong children.' But in the table of contents the same chapter is referred to as having the title, ' To heale the Falling Sicknes : ' thus showing that one and the same sense was attached to both verbs. This use is common enough in Shakespeare :

> Love doth to her eyes repair
> To *help* him of his blindness,
> And being *helpt* inhabits there.—
> > *Two Gent. of Verona*, iv. 2.

a conceit frequently found in the writers of this time, but never more beautifully expressed than here. Again,

> Not *helping*, death's my fee,
> But if I *help*, what do you promise me ?—
> > *All's Well that Ends Well*. i. 2.

> though what it doth impart
> *Help* not at all, but only ease the heart.—*Rich. III.*, iv. 4.

Turn giddy and be *holpe* by backward turning.—*Romeo and Juliet*, i. 2.

Helena, in *All's Well that Ends Well*, undertook, not what we mean by *help*, but the perfect cure of the King. We take one example from Milton ;

> *Helping* all urchin blasts, and ill-luck signs
> That the shrewd meddling elfe delights to make,
> Which she with precious vial'd liquors *heals*.—*Comus*, 845-7.

E

and yet one from Dr. John Hall's *Select Observations upon English Bodies*, 1657 (translated by James Cook),

> and so she was suddenly *helpt*, p. 223.

That this means perfectly cured is shown by the translator's habit of concluding the successful cases in this fashion: 'and so was cured,' p. 176, 'and in a short time became well,' p. 207, 'by which he was wholly delivered,' p. 238. Here, then, we have *help, cure, deliver*, used synonymously.

It is remarkable that this sense of *help*, used by every old English writer on Medicine, should have been unknown to the commentators on Shakespeare. Yet unknown to them it must have been; for otherwise they would not have proposed the emendation of the word in some half-dozen passages which, with one exception, force upon it the medical sense. Let us briefly consider these. In the *Comedy of Errors*, i. 1, the word occurs twice in one line:

> To seek thy *help* by beneficial *help*.

Though the custom of using the word in different senses twice in one line, or even twice in contiguous lines, is not to be commended, it was common at that day. A better example of this could not be found than the line just quoted, or one in *Macbeth*, v. 3,

> Cleanse the *stuff'd* bosom of that perilous *stuff*,

or one in *K. Henry V.*, v. 1:

> To England will I *steal*, and there I'll *steal*.

The late Rev. A. Dyce (*A Few Notes on Shakespeare*, 1853, p. 129) gives a large collection of instances: and a further instalment is contributed by Mr. Marsh, in his *Lectures on the English Language*, Lect. xxv.   We give a few more in a foot-note.[1]

[1] I will come after you, with what good speed
Our means will make us means.—*All's Well that Ends Well.*

If this poor trash of Venice, whom I trash
For his quick hunting.—*Othello*, ii. 1.

These two are cited, with six not in point, by Malone and Steevens, ed. 1821, xi, 253-4.

I'll take my leave
And leave to you the hearing of the cause.—
Measure for Measure, ii. 1.

sound
Their watches on to mine eares the outward watch.—
Richard II., v. 5.

Rain added to a river that is rank
Perforce will force it overflow the bank.—*Venus and Adonis.*

If I could write the beauty of your eyes,
And in fresh numbers number all your graces,
The age to come would say, this poet lies,
Such heavenly touches ne'er toucht earthly faces.—*Sonnet* 17.

Yet some there were, the smaller summe were they,
That joyed to see the summe of all their joy.—
The Countess of Pembrooke's Passion, St. 78 (attributed to Nicholas Breton).

In many places there is the play or the jingle without the repetition : *e. g.*,

I should leave grazing, were I of your flock,
And only live by gazing.—*Winter's Tale*, iv. 3.

Cousins indeed, and by their uncle cozen'd
Of comfort.—*Richard III.*, iv. 4.

Since we have locks to safeguard necessaries,
And pretty traps to catch the petty thieves.—*Henry V.*, i. 2.

Why tender'st thou that paper to me with
A look untender ?—*Cymbeline*, iii. 4.

Such instances must not be confounded with those which constitute Section xliii. of the late W. Sidney Walker's *Critical
Examination of the Text of Shakespeare*, 1860, i. p. 276.   In
the face of so large an induction one might think that no critic
of judgment would have ventured on emendation in the passage
from the *Comedy of Errors*.   It must be taken that the first *help*
means *deliverance*, the second, *succour*.   Yet the line has been
tampered with by Pope, Steevens, Jackson, Collier, Singer, and
Brae.   We spare our readers an account of the nostrums of
the first five.   Mr. A. E. Brae, in his admirable tract, entitled
Collier, Coleridge, and Shakespeare, 1861 (pp. 75 and 150), dis-
cerning with his usual penetration the sense which the passage
ought to carry, proposed to substitute *hele* for *help*, which would
be acceptable enough, but for the fact that *help* means *hele*
(*heal*) already.   It is somewhat curious that *helpful* and *healthful*

Affection is a coal that must be cool'd.—*Venus and Adonis.*

Haply that name of chaste unhapp'ly set
This bateless edge on his keen appetite.—*Lucrece.*

Lean penury within his pen doth dwell,
That to his subjects lends not some small glory.—*Sonnet* 84.

This mist, my friend, is mystical.—*Arden of Feversham.*

I sweare, Aurora, by thy starrie eyes,
And by those golden lockes, whose locke none slips.—
                              Stirling's *Aurora*, Sonnet x.

Still finest wits are stilling Venus' rose.—
                    Southwell's *Saint Peter's Complaint.*

That we may praise them, or themselves prize you.—
                    Herrick.   *To Mildmay, Earl of Warwick.*

And if I trusse not, let me not be trusted.—
                    Chapman.   *Bussy D'Ambois*, iii. 2.

occur before, in the same scene; and that Rowe changed the first into *helpless;* and the editor of the Folio 1632 changed the second into *helpful:* so great a fatality seems to have invested this family of words, all occurring in one scene? Why '*hapless* Ægeon' was not converted by some one into '*hopeless* Ægeon,' and *hopeless* (on its first or second occurrence in that scene) was not converted into *hapless,* may well excite our wonder; that they escaped, our gratitude!

In 2 *Henry VI.,* iv. 7, *help* again occurs, and is again supplanted. Lord Say thus pleads his cause with Jack Cade:

> Long sitting to determine poor men's causes
> Hath made me full of sickness and diseases.

To which Cade replies,

> Ye shall have hempen caudle then, and the *helpe* of hatchet.

Better sense could not be wished: nor do we see how it could be improved in any respect. Cade promises that his lordship's diseases shall be administered-to; he shall have hemp-caudle and hatchet-cure: and if it be thought that Cade's small wit intended a poor quibble here, here it may be found for the seeking; *cord* may be suspected under *caudle,* and *helve* under *helpe,* with a side-glance at the saying 'to throw the helve after the hatchet.' But there is no occasion for this refinement of jest to be found in the passage. Now let us see what the critics have said about it. Farmer, with an eye to the pun, proposed to read *pap* for *help,* and adopts 'of *a* hatchet' from the Folio 1632; which reading Steevens and Ritson admiringly approve, the former saying, 'the help of a hatchet is

little better than nonsense.' But the sense, notwithstanding, is
perfect. Cade proposed to cure Lord Say's sickness by the
aid of 'the sure physician death,' by giving him the rope or
the axe. The article inserted by the editor of the Second
Folio is an impertinence. In *Sonnet* CLIII. we have :

> I, sick withal, the *helpe of bath* desired.

How poor were the sound had he written, 'the helpe of a bath.'
He there meant bath-cure : so in the former case he meant
hatchet-cure. Finally, Mr. A. E. Brae (in the work lately cited,
p. 150) proposed to substitute *hele* for *help* in this place also.
Pap, *helve*, and *hele* agree in this : they carry double : each may
refer to a part of the hatchet, as well as to Lord Say's regimen.
But they also agree in being impertinent, inasmuch as *help* in
the sense of healing is a perfectly satisfactory reading.

The fatality spoken of is not confined to the *Comedy of
Errors* and 2 *Henry VI.* In *All's Well that Ends Well*, i. 3,
we read,

> He and his physicians
> Are of a mind ; he, that they cannot *help* him,
> They, that they cannot *help*.

W. Sidney Walker suggests (with considerable doubt, however,)
that *heal* should supersede the second *help;* and the late Mr.
Samuel Bailey, in contravention of a recognised and accepted
canon, would abolish it in favour of *cure!* Once again, in
2 *Henry VI.*, ii. 1, we have :

> Come, offer at my shrine, and I will *help* thee;

where both Walker and Bailey read *heal* for *help*.

CHAPTER II.

ON THE CORRUPT AND OBSCURE WORDS IN SHAKESPEARE.

IT will be perceived that *help*, *heal*, or *health*, are not mere alternative forms of spelling one word; that in fact we have passed from the case of two such forms to that in which the orthographies belong to two words, coincident in one, at least, of their several significations. *Help* and *heal* are twins, separable as distinct words, yet having the features of a common parent. In Shakespeare we find *bleak* and *bleat* (balare); *break* and *breach* (ruptio); *make* and *mate* (consors); *plait* and *pleach* (intextus); and in other writers *attach* and *attack* (manum inicere); *bak* and *bat* (vespertilio); *moke*, *mote*, and *moth* (blatta); *quilk* and *quilt* (culcita); *reckless* and *retchless* (temerarius); where each pair or set of symbols are equivalents of one and the same word. But words which had once a strictly equivalent usage sometimes grow into synonyms having differences, or even become the signs of distinct words: *e. g.*, *bleak* and *black; dole* and *deal; list* and *lust*, &c.; to which with qualification may be added such pairs or sets of words as *wake, watch*, and *wait; ward* and *guard*,

&c. Then, to crown the work, they may receive some modi-
fication of form by association with cognate, or even incognate
signs.   In this way is the balance of change maintained; for
otherwise the loss, through the inaccurate or careless use of
words, would soon enfeeble and debase the language to such
an extent, that its literature would come to an end, through
failure of the very means of expression.

Such considerations, with a multitude of others which we
cannot set forth in this essay, are of the greatest importance
in the criticism of the text of Shakespeare, particularly where
we have to determine whether a word be interpretable as it
stands, or a corruption demanding emendation.

The risk of applying conjectural criticism to the STILL
LION increases as we proceed with our subject.   Under apparently nonsensical words and phrases often lurk a sense and
intelligence the most 'express and admirable.'   Scarcely a year
passes over our heads but new light, radiating from Elizabethan
lore, shines into some 'dark passage' which the commentator
with his 'farthing candle' has carefully shunned, or the conjectural critic, with his ingenuity and felicity, has tinkered
again and again, and still in vain.   An old author, writing of
the latter, says, 'Hee is the Surgeon of old Authors, and heales
the wounds of dust and ignorance' (*Micro-Cosmographie*, 1628,
§ 35).   If he did, it would be hard to denounce him for probing
them.   The complaint, however, is just this, that he does not
heal them.   His surgery not unfrequently is butchery; but of
the healing art he knows as little as a barber-surgeon.   There
is an old 'jeast' of such a one who, having to shave a cus-

tomer, fell to cursing, because he cut his thumb, which he had put in his patient's cheek to force it out tense and firm. Happily, Shakespearian barber-surgeons sometimes do this too, and, sadder or wiser by experience, handle their author with more feeling for the future, or leave him alone. But though some notable cures have been performed, notwithstanding, by the regulars of criticism, there yet remain, after all, a number of corrupt places which have persistently failed to profit by their nostrums. Of single words thus situated there are some thirty which thus get referred to the category of *immortal nonsense.*

First, as to textual difficulties affecting single words. Here are a sheaf of these 'ugly customers,' with most of whom every conscientious editor has played a losing game.

An-heires. Merry Wives of Windsor, ii. 1.
Arm-gaunt. Antony and Cleopatra, i. 5.
Aroint. Macbeth, i. 3. Lear, iii. 4.
Barlet. Macbeth, i. 6.
Bone. Timon of Athens, iii. 5.
Charge-house. Love's Labours Lost, v. 2.
Cars. Twelfth Night, ii. 5.
Cyme. Macbeth, v. 3.
Ducdame. As You Like It, ii. 5.
Dung. Antony and Cleopatra, v. 2.

Empirickqutick. Coriolanus, ii. 1.
Esil. Hamlet, v. 1.
Land-damn. Winter's Tale, ii. 1.
Oneyers. 1 Hen. IV, ii, 1.
Paiocke. Hamlet, iii, 2.
Prenzie. Measure for Measure, iii, 1.
Runaways. Romeo and Juliet, iii, 2.
Scamels. Tempest, ii, 1.
Skains-mates. Romeo and Juliet, ii, 4.
Strachy. Twelfth Night, ii, 5.
Vllorxa. Timon of Athens, iii, 3.
Yaughan. Hamlet, v, 1.

From the penultimate word we will call the entire class *Ullorxals.*

We must allow, at the outset, that few of these strange

F

words are utterly hopeless; that one or two will trouble no
one's peace any longer; and that some bid fair to justify themselves, or to reveal, through their corruption, the true words
which, owing to the blunder of reader, writer, or compositor,
suffered this perversion.   One can hardly doubt that *aroint* is
a true word, though it has been often attacked and defended
with great pertinacity, ingenuity, and learning.   But, though a
true word, its exact sense or root-meaning has not been ascer-
tained.   It has been thought to mean, *be off*, from the A. S.:
and either *get thee behind*, or *plague take thee*, or *break thy back*,*
from the French.   But anyhow, the phrase, *rynt thee*, occurs
in an old proverb.†   *Barlet* was corrected by the editor of
the folio 1632; it is a press-error for *Martlet*.‡   *Cyme* has been
thought to be a misprint for *cené*, an obsolete form of *senna :*
but the researches of Mr. H. A. J. Munro have pretty nearly
established the right of *cyme* to its place in the text.   It appears
to be κῦμα, *cyma*, the name given by Galen, Celsus, Columella,

---

* But *éreinte-toi* (literally *break thy back*) would not be applied to a
witch, whose instant flight is the *desideratum*.

† Mrs. Browning has,

> ' Whisker'd cats *arointed* flee,

and we observe in the *Animal World*, vol. v., p. 23,

> ' What wonder that the vermin fled *arointed*.'

From these expressions one would infer that *aroint* is extant in some
northern dialect.   We have heard *squander* applied to vermin in this very
way by a Yorkshireman.   *Aroint* is used by Sir W. Scott : 'wherefore
aroint ye, if ye were ten times my master, unless ye come in bodily shape,
lith and limb.—*Bride of Lammermoor*, ch. vii.

‡ Just as we have *Barlows* for *Marlows* in Richard Carew's *Excellencie
of the English Tongue* (Camden's *Remaines*, 1614).

Vertomannus, &c., to the early sprouts of cabbage, which was commonly used as a gentle purgative.* *Arm-gaunt* is assuredly a misprint; for if such a word was ever applied to a horse in the sense of *gaunt in the forequarters*, such a horse would, in Shakespeare's phrase, be almost *shoulder-shotten:* and most certainly Anthony's high-bred charger could not have been that. Either *arrogant, rampaunt,* or *tarmagaunt* is a more likely correction than *armgirt,* which has been confidently proposed : but *nostro judicio, termagant* would be a poor, if not an inappropriate epithet for the charger. The article *an,* as Singer observes, is in favour of *arrogant. Charge-house* is, almost certainly, *church-house,* and the mis-spelling may be intentional to indicate the pronunciation, just as in *Much Ado About Nothing,* Dogberry's *losses* may have been intended for *law-suits.* On the other hand, was there ever such a word as *charge-house,* for *domus curationis?* Or is *charge* a misprint for *cleargie?* *Scamels* has hitherto presented an irreducible crux, and ten substitutes for it have been proposed. But we are happy to be able to state that at length it has shown some title to its prescriptive place in the text. Norfolk, a *scamel* is the name for the female *pick:* this being the male of *Limosa rufa,* or the Bar-tailed Godwit. (See Stevenson's *Birds of Norfolk,* vol. ii. p. 260.) Still, we are not aware of such birds frequenting the rocks for

* Philemon Holland, in his version of Pliny, employs the plural *cymes,* where Pliny has the singular, *cyma:* 'Yet none put foorth their *cymes* or tender buds more than they [*i. e.,* the colewort].' Holland's Pliny, 1601 : ii. p. 25; again, 'Of all kinds of Coleworts, the sweetest and most pleasant to the tast, is the Col-florie *cyma* [in margin], although it be counted good for nothing in Physicke.' But on this point doctors disagreed.

breeding.* *Esil* is either *Eysell* (*i. e.*, vinegar, or worm-wood wine), or the name of a Danish river *(Yssel)*. *Bone*, one of the most senseless corruptions in all Shakespeare, escaped unchallenged, strange to say, till Mr. Staunton made two unlucky guesses at it in his edition of Shakespeare. It appears to be a misprint for *bed*, the termination *one* (instead of *ed*) having been caught from *onely* or from *none* in the same line. Assuredly it was *there*, and there only, that Alcibiades would have wished to prolong the lives of the senators, who were already prepared by their servile imbecility for being put away out of sight. Of *runaways* we shall have somewhat to say hereafter. Guesses enow have been made at the words for which the rest in our sheaf may have been press-errors : but with the exception of *Empirickqutick*, *skains-mates*, and *Vaughan*, they all remain to this day shrouded in hopeless obscurity. As to these three, *Vaughan* may be a proper-name; and if such a name be not found in records of the time, it may well be a misprint for either Vaughan or Johan, which would be the tapster's name. *Skain*, Mr. Staunton tells us, used to be heard in the Isle of Thanet, in the sense of scapegrace ; but we do not agree with him that this fact removes all difficulty with the word. *Empirickqutick*, till the advent of the Perkins-imposture, was always turned into *empiric* or *empirick*, and, we think, rightly so. It seems clear that *Empirickqutick* belongs to a very definite class of misprints, which we may call *duplicative*. Here are a

* We are indebted to Dr. R. G. Latham for this reference. We did not take it from the note at page 120 of the Clarendon Press edition of *The Tempest*, where the same explanation is given and the same objection taken.

few examples of the class, observed by the writer:—*Respec-tivective* for *respective*, in the office-copy of a will : *axiomomata* for *axiomata*, in Whewell's *Philosophy of Discovery*, 1860, p. 144 : *Aurorora* for *Aurora*, in *The English Parnassus*, 1657, p. 400 : *Blakelesley* for *Blakesley* in Reeves and Turner's *Catalogue*, No. 253 : *Thackerary* for *Thackeray* in Salkeld's *Catalogue*, No. 112 : *Concannon-street* for *Cannon-street*, in *The Times* of March 16, 1875 : and *puriritie* for *puritie*, in the first folio of Shakespeare. And still more to the purpose the following : 'the whiche * * they adjudged for *prognostiqukys* and tokens of the Kynges deth:' in Fabyan's *Chronicle*, vol. i. c. 246 : where the word *prognostiquykys* is a misprint for *pronostiques*. This is an error of near kin to *Empirickqutick;* and exemplifies the tendency of writers and compositors to repeat some syllable in a word which is susceptible of two forms of spelling : as, in this case, with a *qu*, or a *ck*. In practice we have often found ourselves anticipating the terminal consonants of the next word, in the one we happened to be writing : as *make work* for *may work; make speak* for *may speak;* and so forth : and in the first edition of *The Still Lion*, at p. 209 of the *Jahrbuch*, the former error of writing was actually made in the copy, and set up, without being subsequently detected : whereby a second misprint was grafted upon a line in *The Tempest*, as if in com-pensation for losing the one we had it in hand to expose and correct. So it came to pass that the very page containing our remarks on duplicative errors, presented an example of the very kind. Of the residue of the words in our sheaf, nearly all of which are mere printer's sphinx-riddles, *ducdame* (which, like

aroint and *prenzie,* has the distinguished honour of occurring
more than once in the text of Shakespeare) has been regarded
as a nonsensical refrain ; and in support of that view Mr. J.
O. Phillips (Halliwell) cites, from the burden of an old song,
dusadam-me-me. But such refrains are common enough ; and
if one could only be sure that *ducdame* is no more than *such* a
refrain, one would not be solicitous about its pedigree. Allowing
it to be such a refrain, and therefore one in which no meaning
would be looked for, is it likely that Amiens would have been
made to show such solicitude about it ?   Had it been, for
instance, *dan-dyry-cum-dan,* thrice repeated, would Shakespeare
have made him ask Jaques, ' What's that *dan-dyry-cum-dan ?* '
Surely not.

CHAPTER III.

ON THE DIFFICULT PHRASES IN SHAKESPEARE, AND THE DANGER OF TAMPERING WITH THEM.

BUT the critic is in danger of assuming, on insufficient evidence, that not a word only, but an entire sentence, owes its obscurity to the corruption of words by scribes and printers. It is convenient to consider phrases under three heads: *idioms, idiotisms,* and *idiasms:* which may be briefly explained as follows :—

All living languages are in a state of continuous change. Not only do words fall into disuse, and others accrue to the general stock, not only do the orthographical forms in which they are presented to the eye undergo change, but each several word is ever more or less changing its meaning, both in scope and in force. Some words (like *shy, secure*) obtain a signification directly contrary to their former meaning; or (like *let, prevent*) retain two contrary meanings at once. Others (like *knave, piece, lewd*) pass from a respectable to a disreputable sense; while others (like *liberty, practice, occupy,** convey*) throw

---

* 'A captain! These villains will make the word "captain" as odious as the word "occupy," which was an excellent good word before it was ill-sorted.'— 2 *Hen. IV.*, ii. 4. This word is now restored to its old respectability.

off their disreputable association, and become honourable symbols of speech. The literal sense of some gives way to the
figurative, and, perhaps more rarely, the reverse; and a word
which has done duty as one part of speech becomes another.
But not only do words thus change; but all kinds of expression
written and spoken change also. The normal affinities of parts
of speech constitute the *idiom :* the singular phrase, which does
not conform to the idiomatic construction, is the *idiotism.*
There remain phrases and words peculiar to some creative
writer; these we call *idiasms* (ἰδιασμοί). Thus it appears that
the *idiom* is a regular, the *idiotism* a proverbial, and the *idiasm* a
private and peculiar mode of phraseology. At present we shall
confine our remarks to complete sentences, and the changes
and corruptions of sentences; passing by that intermediate
class of corruptions which involve several words, but not an
entire phrase.

The idioms of a language change, but slowly, under dialec-
tical and colloquial influences; and apart from those influences,
scarcely change at all. But idiotisms are constantly slipping
out as pedantries, and creeping in as slang. Shakespeare's
works, like all the literature of his day, as might be expected,
contain many idioms which by this time have become obsolete
or dead. The worst of it is, that we read him so much, and
with so little appropriate knowledge and steady reflection, that
we get habituated to the look and sound of his phraseology,
and come at last to think we understand it, mistaking the
familiar for the intelligible. The same has come to pass of
the Authorised Version of the Holy Scriptures. Such an idiom

as is involved in the sentence, 'I do the [thee] to wytene [under-
stand] that it is made be [by] enchauntement,' in Maundevile's
Voiage and Travaile (A.D. 1322-46), is as dead as a door-nail :
yet we have the same, 'We do you to wit of the grace of God,'
in the A. V. ; and we read this over and over again, and get
so used to it, that it comes upon us as the voice of an old
familiar friend, while it is as unintelligible as an unknown
tongue, and was obsolescent when King James' Bible was
first printed. How often, too, have we read the lines in
Hamlet, v. 2,

> Does it not, think thee, stand me now upon,
>   * * * *   is't not perfect conscience,
> To quit him with this arm ?

but to how many readers is this idiotism intelligible ? For
one thing, that passage is absurdly pointed in most editions
of the play ; the true construction being, that the idiotism
in question governs the infinitive, 'To quit (requite) him with
this arm.' The same expression is employed in three other
places in Shakespeare : viz., *Rich. II.*, ii. 3 ; *Rich. III.*, iv. 2 ;
and *Antony and Cleopatra*, ii. 1. See also *Romeo and Juliet*,
ii. 3 ('I stand on sudden haste'— but which is not *identical*
with the expression in question). It is usually explained cor-
rectly in annotated editions ; but the editors satisfy themselves
by quoting from other parts of Shakespeare in illustration of it.
We give two contemporary examples from other works :

Then they are worthy to be hanged eternally in Hel, that will not most
gladly, * * * come to heare the eternall God the King of heaven himselfe speake, who doth pronounce, &c., &c. . . . which to heare, marke,

G

remember, and observe, *it stands us upon.*—Lupton's *Too good to be true.*
1580, p. 25.

> It was concealed, and therefore *stands upon*,
> Whether through our advice you will be saved,
> Or in his beastly entrails be en-graved.
>   *Cupid and Psyche*, by Shakerley Marmion, 1637.

Again, how often have we read that inimitable scene in
2 *Hen. IV.*, i. 2, where Falstaff says of his mercer,

> A whoreson Achitophel! a rascally yea-forsooth knave! *to bear* a gen-
> tleman *in hand*, and then stand upon security.

This idiotism also occurs in six other places in Shakespeare : viz., *The Taming of the Shrew*, iv. 2 ; *Much Ado About
Nothing*, iv. 1 ; *Measure for Measure*, i. 4 ; *Cymbeline*, v. 5 ;
Macbeth, iii. 1 ; *Hamlet*, ii. 2.   Examples of this are commoner
in Elizabethan literature, than of the former.   Here are five :

> There be many diseases in the bodies of men and beasts which he
> [the Devil] seeth will breake foorth unto lamenesse or unto death, he
> *beareth* the Witches *in hand* he doth them.
> Giffard's *Dialogue Concerning Witches and Witchcrafts*, 1603. The Epistle.

> And yet much worse is it to make them to mary by striving and hate,
> threatning, and sute : as when they goe to lawe together, the man for
> the woman, *bearing* her *in hand* that shee is his wife :—Vives' *Instruc-
> tion of a Christian Woman* (R. Hyrd), 1592.   Sig. N 2.

> And as for the manner of his Apostacy or backsliding, the priest
> himselfe, nay the partie himselfe, nay we our selves know to be farre
> otherwise then they woulde faine here *beare* us *in hand*.—Racster, 1598,
> last page.

> And againe, those which being hitherto *borne in hande* that men's soules
> returne againe on earth, * * * will confesse the like.—*Of Ghostes
> and Spirites*, 1596.   To the Reader.

Salomon teacheth us to chasten children with the rod, and so to make them stand in awe : he doth not say, we must *beare* them *in hand* they shall be devoured of Bugges, Hags of the night, and such like monsters.—*Ibid*, p. 21.

(It also occurs at pp. 27, 31, 32, 53, 187, 210, and 211 of this curious and instructive treatise, which is a translation of the well-known work, *De Lemuribus*, of Lavaterus ; and it is common in Ben Jonson, Heywood, and the early dramatists.) The phrase is of great antiquity. The earliest example that has come under our notice is in Drant's *Horace's Sat.* (Sig. A ii.), 1566, but is there in the form *to hold one in hand* in the sense of *persuade*, simply. As to the meaning of these idiotisms, *To stand upon* is to be incumbent on. *To bear in hand* is to inspire misplaced confidence or belief.

It were easy to multiply to any extent examples of obsolete idiotism : for further illustrations take these four : *to die and live by a thing; to remember one's courtesy ; to cry on a thing; to cry game;* all of which have been mercilessly handled by the editors and commentators. In cases where a few examples of the phrase have been discovered in contemporary literature the love of emendation has yielded to the force of evidence. Where that evidence cannot be adduced the suspected phrase falls an easy prey to 'conjectural felicity,' *i. e.,* to barbarous innovation.

The slow and comparatively slight changes which the true idioms of the language have undergone, do, in fact, occasion the critic no difficulty. The expression *No is ?* (for *Is not ?*), *No did ? No have ?* is a totally obsolete idiom ; one instance of which occurs in Shakespeare, viz., in *King John*, iv. 2, where

' No had ' of the Folio has been usually altered into *Had none*.
(See *Notes and Queries*, 1st S. vii. 520 & 593.)   The use of the
relative absolute (with active or neuter participles) was in
use as late as Locke : at least three instances of it are in
Shakespeare : viz., two in *The Tempest*, i. 2 ('*Who having*, &c.,
he did believe,' &c.   'A noble Neapolitan, &c., *who being*,'
&c., did give us '), and one in *Love's Labours Lost*, i. 1 ('*Who
dazzling* so, that eye shall be,' &c.), in the first of which the
seeming solecism has given occasion to several emendations.*
The suppression of the relative as subject was almost as normal a usage as its expression ; and in some half-dozen places
in Shakespeare, where such is the construction, the text has
been conjecturally altered.   But above all other peculiarities
of the Elizabethan idiom was that of inflectional conjugation,
e. g., the use of the third person plural in *s* or *th*, which in
the case of Shakespeare has been almost always regarded as
a grammatical inaccuracy !   Some critics have gone so far as
to reflect on Shakespeare's imperfect education, and to attempt
the poor joke, that if, as Mr. Halliwell asserts, he did go
to Stratford Grammar School, he must have learnt anything
but grammar !   Another explains the apparent irregularities in
Shakespeare by the supposition that ' the thought blew the

---

   * After all is it certain that these are all instances of 'the relative
absolute'? at least one ('Who having into truth,' &c.) looks like a case
of 'the supplementary pronoun.' (See Abbott's *Shakespearean Grammar*,
1870, § 249.) c f.

> Which when it bites and blows, &c., I smile and say,
> This is no flattery. —*As You Like It*, ii. 1.

language to shivers,' which, it appears, is a natural character-
istic of literary genius! Accordingly it has been deemed an
act of kindness to cure him of those defects. So it has happened that the editors have corrected his grammar, as well as
modernized his spelling; but in doing this they have betrayed
an amount of ignorance for which they would not otherwise
have had the discredit. THE STILL LION HAS BEEN AMPLY
AVENGED ON HIS FOES.

After all that a sound knowledge of English Literature, and
of the evolution of the English Language, with the concurrence of conjectural skill, can effect in vindicating and restoring
the genuine text of Shakespeare, there still remain a number
of corruptions which, like the Ullorxals, are mere printers'
Sphinx-riddles. These, however, unlike the Ullorxals, consist
of several entire words, and are cases not so much of corrupt
words as of corrupt phrases; and, while it is possible that some
of these are pure idiasms, it is much more probable that they
are idiotisms of the time or textual corruptions. Among this
numerous family are the following, which will serve as samples of the class:

1.　　I see that men make ropes in such a scarre
　　　That we'll forsake ourselves.
　　　　　　　　　　All's Well that Ends Well, iv. 2.

2.　　　　　　　　　　　It is as lawful,
　　　For we would count give much to as violent thefts
　　　And rob in the behalf of charity.—*Troilus and Cressida*, v. 3.

3.　　　　　　　　　The dram of eale
　　　Doth all the noble substance of a doubt
　　　To his own scandal.—*Hamlet*, i. 4.

4.   That I had no angry wit to be a lord.
                              Timon of Athens, i. 1.

5.   I would they would forget me, like the virtues
       Which our divines lose by 'em.—*Coriolanus*, ii. 3.

6.   Which sleeps, and never palates more the dung,
       The beggars Nurse, and Cæsar's.
                              Antony and Cleopatra, v. 2.

From the first of these examples, I call the family *Rope-scarres*. In dealing with these the success of the critic has been infinitesimally small. We are indebted to the collations in the Cambridge Edition of Shakespeare (supplemented by the editors' manuscript collections which have been placed at our disposal) for the numbers in the following table. If these numbers do not fairly represent the relative difficulty of these passages, they will at least testify to the absolute difficulty of all, and to the ill success that has rewarded criticism. It should be borne in mind here, that to the obscurity of the passage must be added the dulness of the critic. The difficulty may lie, as in fact it often does, as much in the perceptions of the recipient, as in the obscurity of the phraseology to be received.

1,	19	conjectures.	4,	15	conjectures.
2,	15	,,	5,	6	,,
3,	47	,,	6,	7	,,

It would be a thankless task to specify the actual number of Rope-scarres in the entire text of Shakespeare. The list is considerable: but to our mind, the wonder is that the text is, on the whole, so free from misprisions and dislocations.

When we consider the misprints which disfigure modern books, even those which have received the most vigilant and jealous supervision, both of Editor and of Reader, it is to be expected that, at a time when printing was not conducted on so methodical a plan as at present, and when important works were generally issued without any regular editorial supervision, the first Edition of Shakespeare should exhibit a harvest of typographical casualties. On the whole we are disposed to regard that edition as being quite as free from typographical errors as the majority of dramatic works of that time. Moreover, we are convinced that much of the obstinate intractability of these Rope-scarres is due to the intermixture of obsolete phrases, Shakespearian idiasms, or forgotten allusions, with certain typographical errors ; so that it is not surprising that the conjectural critic should find himself unable to set them right by the mere exercise of his ingenuity and taste.

CHAPTER IV.

AN EXAMINATION AND DEFENSE OF CERTAIN WORDS
AND PHRASES IN SHAKESPEARE, WHICH HAVE
SUFFERED THE WRONGS OF EMENDATION.

THE three foregoing chapters are intended rather for warning than for the value of the criticisms which they contain. Let us now apply ourselves to a selection of passages, which have received the doubtful benefit of conjectural emendation. Our warning has been somewhat prolix; but our best excuse will be found in the treatment to which portions of the ancient text of Shakespeare have been subjected at the hands of his censors and critics. So capricious are the objections preferred against particular words and phrases, that it is a sheer impossibility to anticipate them. Accordingly the antiquarian of the English Language, who essays the vindication of the old text, stands at a great disadvantage. To learn the acknowledged peculiarities and difficulties of that text is a labour of love; and to retain all the salient points of Shakespeare's phraseology in an ever ready and lively memory is but a light prelude to the business that is to follow. With these matters ever consciously before him—'full of eyes before and behind'—the critic wades through a huge store of the literature of the sixteenth and seventeenth centuries, noting down every word, phrase, and illusion, which can by any possibility throw light on the text of his venerated author. This is the toil which has been achieved by all the leading editors from Steevens to Dyce, with a few exceptions, which it is as well to forget. Fit propædeutic is such a course of study and discipline to the more genial and graceful duties of verbal criticism! The labour achieved, the preliminary requirement complied with at the cost of much time and effort, some vain reader, of blissful ignorance but of lively fancy, conceives a liking for what he pleasantly regards as the *game* of criticism, and rushes into the columns of some periodical, such as the *Athenæum*, or *Notes and Queries*, to proclaim with flourish of trumpets a new reading. His conjecture is, as a matter of course, described as 'the undoubted restoration of a passage which has for two centuries and a half defied alike exposition and correction.' Then follows, equally as a matter of course, the discovery of a mare's nest. The would-be critic has mistaken the sense of a passage both well known and perfectly understood; whereupon he proposes what he takes for a new conjecture, but which in many cases is an old and not very creditable acquaintance, whose familiar features may be seen recorded in some *variorum hortus siccus*, under the sanction of a venerable name. In a few of such cases it is no great tax upon the antiquarian to produce his authority for adhering to the old text: but where there are so many 'Richmonds in the field,' he naturally and reason-

H

ably grudges the superfluous labour of defending what is impregnable. He rightly feels that faith in the prodigious learning of a Walker or a Dyce is a simple duty with learners; and that for them to put a word or phrase on its trial merely because they 'don't seem to see it,' is an impertinence, against which every well-informed and competent editor would jealously guard his columns. In some cases, however, the vindication of a challenged expression in Shakespeare is inconclusive, by reason of the very absurdity of the challenge. We have more than once seen an expression denounced as senseless, which assuredly had never occasioned the slightest difficulty with any one; and for this very reason no critic had ever thought it worth while to register the instances of its use which had occurred in the course of his reading. We ourselves have noticed a peculiarity of language occurring over and over again, of which we did not stop to record a single example, because its employment by Shakespeare had never provoked remark, and seemed unable to afford a foothold for suspicion. Yet we have lived to see the passage in which it occurred obelized as an 'unsuspected corruption,' and to find ourselves incapacitated, through the want of superhuman prescience, for the work of vindication. It is impossible to stop every cranny against the aggression of a misplaced ingenuity, which 'infects unseen,' and corrupts the text it seems to restore.

As the inquiry we are about to institute is 'of the dust dusty' in its extreme dryness and in the antiquity of the literature from which we shall draw our illustrations, we will preface it with a couple of relevant anecdotes. As both are derived from the store of our forgetive friend, Mr. Perkins-Ireland, we will not vouch for their literal truth. He tells us that a literary bore of his acquaintance came to him one day with a pocket-edition of Shakespeare, in which a well-known line in *King John* thus stood :

'Bel, Booke, and Candle shall not *course* me back.'

The bore was swelled with the importance of a critical discovery: his 'business looked out of him.' He triumphantly pointed to the line, in which over the antepenult he had written the word, *curse*. '*Course*,' said he decisively, 'must be a misprint for *curse*.' Mr. Perkins-Ireland was taken aback by the apparent felicity of the conjecture, but promptly asked his friend for his proofs: who thereupon produced an extract from page 17 of Lupton's *Too Good To Be True* (an ominous title!), which ran thus :

'The best thing the Pope can do is to *curse* him out again, with Bel, Booke, and Candle.'

This he followed up with another from page 23 of *Ariosto's Seven Planets Governing Italie*,

'Then roares the bulles worse then the Basan host, Whilst Belles and bookes and candles *curses* boast.'

This he was following up with others: when Mr. Perkins-Ireland stopped him, and pointed out that one thing was yet unproved, that *curse* was ever spelt *course*. His friend was naturally indignant at so discomforting a requisition: for if *course* was just *curse* under an archaic orthography, the credit to be awarded to the bore was of a very different kind, he thought

of an inferior kind, to that he claimed: he would be no
longer the emender, but the exponent of the word in the text.
But whether he would or no, the thing was virtually done for
him: for Mr. Perkins-Ireland himself found *course* spelt *curse*
in Leland, and *scourge* spelt *scurge* in Richard Hyrd and George
Chapman ; so he frankly owned that his friend had, at least,
invested the passage in *King John* with a new and most admirable
sense.   Their triumphal rejoicings, however, were of very short
duration.   Fortunately, before breaking up the conference, Mr.
Perkins-Ireland, with his well-known caution, had the prudence
to turn to his *Variorum.*   There, to his and his friend's astonish-
ment, he found the line in *King John* printed thus:—

'Bell, Book and Candle shall not *drive* me back;'

and so it stood in half-a-dozen other editions at hand.   Obviously
his friend's pocket-edition was, at least in that line, misprinted;
and he departed chap-fallen at this new discovery, that he had
been bringing his critical resources to bear on a word which
was not in Shakespeare's text !

That's not a bad anecdote: but here's a better.   Both enforce
the lesson, 'look before you leap.'   It is as dangerous to criticize
a passage without consulting the context, as it is to do so
without verifying it.   Mr. Perkins-Ireland was the critic in this
case.   He was reading *Much Ado About Nothing*, ii. 1 (another
ominous title !), when he came upon the passage,

'and then comes repentance, and, with his bad legs, falls into the cinque-
pace faster and faster, till he sink [apace] into his grave.'

The addition of *apace* was made by his cousin, Mr. Thomas

Perkins, of Folio 1632 celebrity; and Mr. Perkins-Ireland thought it eminently ingenious. 'But,' said he to himself, 'What is the meaning of *cinque-pace* ? Surely it must be some sort of disease : in fact, the whole passage reminds one of Falstaff's *degrees* of sickness and wickedness, which my cousin Thomas so rashly altered into *diseases.*' Thereupon he took down his copy of Andrew Boord's *Breviarie of Health,* and to his delight found a disease called the *Sinkopis,* the description of which accorded admirably with that of Repentance, 'with his bad legs,' sinking into his grave. It is not to be wondered at that he believed himself to have hit upon a capital emendation. But for all that, his caution did not desert him; and he once more applied himself to the text, this time reading it with the context; and on perceiving that Beatrice had just said, 'Wooing, wedding, and repenting, is as a Scotch jig, a measure, and a *cinque-pace,*' began to be ashamed of his precipitation, if not of his ingenuity. The fact is, that emendation is always a ticklish business. THE CRITIC CAN NEVER TELL WHETHER THE LION IS DEAD, ASLEEP, OR ONLY SHAMMING SLEEP. HE TAKES A DEAL OF WALKING-ROUND, AND TICKLING WITH A LONG STRAW, AND POKING WITH A STICK, BEFORE ONE CAN BE REASON-ABLY SURE THAT IT IS SAFE TO COME TO CLOSE QUARTERS WITH HIM.

We will now proceed to consider in detail a dozen selected characteristics of Shakespearian criticism.

1. It is remarkable that it is not the most difficult passages in Shakespeare that have occasioned the greatest dispute: on the contrary, the most hotly contested questions relate to pas-

sages of which the only fault in the eyes of a competent critic is, that the sense is perhaps too obvious. No one, attentively considering such passages, can fail to find *some* sense, though perhaps every one feels that after all *the* sense intended by Shakespeare has eluded his vigilance, and believes that something better remains to be found *in* the text, or, failing that, to be found *for* it. In such speculation, whether of investigation or of tentative substitution, there is, on the whole, much good; provided the critic does not overlook what is 'under his nose,' which is, in so many places, the very meaning which ought to put a term to speculation. Here is an example in point. Juliet, impatiently awaiting the advent of Romeo to her nuptial couch, thus invokes the night :—

> Spred thy close Curtaine Love-performing night,
> That run-awayes eyes may wincke, and *Romeo*
> Leape to these armes, untalkt of and unseene.
>
> *Romeo and Juliet*, iii. 2.

So the folio 1623, and two of the quarto editions, the two earlier quartos reading *runnawayes*. For this word *run-awayes*, which was not suspected till after Capell's edition, and which admits of explanation without the least *tour de force*, we find that no less than thirty-two substitutes have been proposed, whereof seven have been inserted in the text of as many editions! As we do not intend to furnish a list of conjectural readings for any other passage, we will do so in this case, merely to show with what fatuous imbecility the conjectural critics would fain over-ride the diction of Shakespeare, wherever it happens to be obscured by archaism or weakened by seeming platitude.

First, however, we must premise that there was such a substantive as *runaway*, and that, in the language of the time, it was for the whole gamut of its meaning the same as *runagate*, with which every English Churchman is familiar from the version of the Psalms appended to the Liturgy. But when it is said that JEHOVAH 'letteth the *runagates* continue in scarceness,' the persons who are so let to starve are *delinquents*, those who are *runaways* from duty, who habitually *run away* from or *desert* the cause they are bound to support. Arthur Golding thus employs both *runagates* and *runaways*, to describe those who have deserted the enemy's camp, and come over to Cæsar's. But the senses of *delinquent* and *deserter* are special senses alike of *runagate* and of *runaway*. The more general signification of either word is, one who having treacherously acquired anything (news or goods), makes off with it, *runs away* to escape detection and appropriate what he has so obtained. In this sense Shakespeare may very well have used the word in *Romeo and Juliet*. But again, vagabonds who haunt the streets towards dusk for dishonest purposes might be very well called *runagates* or *runaways*. It will be observed that the textual word 'run-awayes' may stand either for *runaways'* or for *runaway's;* and if satisfactory sense can be made of either, surely emendation is an impertinence. Mr. N. J. Halpin, in a remarkable essay printed among the *Shakespeare Society's Papers* and called ' The Bridal Runaway,' has made out a very strong case for the latter form, taking Runaway as the epithalamial sobriquet of Love. But if that view should be decided against, we have still the former, which, as we have shown, admits of ample justification. Our own impression is that Shakespeare is using the word as a plural possessive—*runaways' eyes.* He might, for the sense, have just as well employed *runagates':* but not for the verse; for though in *runagates'* he would have preserved the symptosis of the *run* and *Rom,* he would have lost that of the *ways'* and *wink.*

But not only is *runaways'* defensible, but it is easily shown to be the appropriate word for the place. Juliet says,

> Spred thy close Curtaine Love-performing night,
> That run-awayes eyes may winke,———

What eyes? To answer which question we must determine what eyes are made to wink, or are deprived of their function, *as a consequence* of the advent of Night. Shakespeare might have used a very reprehensible metaphor, and spoken of Day's *eyes,* as some of his contemporaries did: but the winking of Day's eyes, and the closure of Night's curtain, are one and the same thing, not distinct operations of which the one is dependent upon the other. So, despite Mr. Dyce's deliverances, *those* eyes are excluded from the possibilities of the case. Shakespeare might also, and with great propriety, have spoken of Night's eyes, meaning the stars; but unless by *wink* he meant *twinkle,* the closure of Night's curtain, so far from being the condition upon which the stars are made to wink, or are veiled, is in fact the only occasion of their shining forth: so Night's eyes are equally excluded. Despite Walker and Mitford, no poet speaks of the Moon's *eyes;* but if Shakespeare had ever done so, he would not have done so here; for the advent of Night only serves to make her brighter. Lastly, can the eyes alluded to be those of either or both of the lovers. To answer this we must consider the next line :

> That runawayes eyes may winke, and *Romeo*
> Leape to these armes, untalkt of and unseene,

from which it appears that the winking of those eyes is the condition precedent of Romeo's security from detection : and it would be an insult to common sense to inquire whether the closing of Juliet's eyes, or of Romeo's eyes, could contribute to that result. Similarly, the twinkling of the stars, brought out by the approach of night, could not help to insure Romeo's immunity from suspicion ; so that cannot be the winking contemplated by Shakespeare. We are thus driven into a corner, and are obliged to find the objects connoted by *runaways* in those who, but for the darkness, might spy out the approach of the lover, and betray the secret to parties interested in the frustration of his design.*

There is nothing unusual, recondite, or far-fetched, in this explanation : yet the bulk of the critics will not have it. Does it make one blush for mortal dulness that such a passage should have been singled out for almost exhaustive emendation? Perhaps the best way of presenting these conjectures is to classify them under the leading conceptions which gave them birth.

---

* Mr. F. J. Furnivall takes this view in a letter in the *Academy* (March 21, 1874). After quoting *Fugitif*, *Roder*, *Rodeur*, &c., from Cotgrave, 1611. he concludes, 'Shakspere's runawayes, runagates, or runabouts, were the *rodeurs des rues* with a different object, men who'd leave no young lovers "vntalkt of and vnseene," while the light lasted.'

I

(1) It is conceived that *run-awayes* is a misprint for the proper name of the source or sources of daylight, moonlight, or starlight. Hence we are favoured with five conjectures: *Luna's,* Mitford: *Cynthia's,* Walker: *Uranus',* Anon.: *Titan's,* Bullock: *wandering* (*wandering eyes* being the planets. *Athenæum,* August 6, 1870).

(2) It is conceived that *run-awayes* is a misprint for some word of which the last syllable is *day's.* This gives us four more: *rude day's* and *soon day's,* Dyce: *sunny day's,* Clarke: *noonday's,* Anon.

(3) It is conceived that *run-awayes* is a misprint for the name of a mythical person. This gives us four more: *th' Runaway's* (*i. e.,* the Sun), Warburton: *the runaway's,* Capell: *Rumour's,* Heath: *Renomy's* (*i. e., Rénommée*), Mason.

(4) It is conceived that the first syllable of *run-awayes* is a misprint for *sun.* This gives us four, one being already mentioned. *Sun away,* Taylor: *sun-awake's,* Brady: *sun-aweary,* McIlwaine: *sunny day's,* Clarke (as before).*

(5) It is conceived that the misprint is in the last syllable only of *run-awayes.* This gives us five more: *runagate's,* Beckett: *run-away,* Blackstone: *run-astray,* Taylor: *run-abouts',* Keightley: *runaway spies,* H. K.

(6) It is conceived that *ware* or *wary,* formed part of the word for which *run-awayes* stands. This gives us three more. *Unawares,* Jackson: *unwary,* Taylor: *waryones',* Anon.

(7) A class to which we may assign various conjectures which

---

* On seeing this proof Mr. Perkins-Ireland maliciously asks whether any one has ever proposed to read *Grundy's eyes.*

do not fall in the other six. We have *rumourous* and *ru-mourers'*, Singer: *enemies*, Collier: *roavinge*, Dyce: *yonder*, Leo: *ribalds* and *roaming*, Anon.: *Veronese* (*Nation*, May, 1871); amounting to eight more:

on which miscellaneous repast, of both the wholesome and the baneful, we may well ask one blessing—a speedy deliverance from one and all.

2. We sometimes meet with a conventional phrase or idiotism employed by Shakespeare in a sense peculiar to himself, *i. e.*, as an idiasm. The following example is most instructive. We quote from *As You Like It*, iii. 5 (Folio 1623).

> the common executioner
> Whose heart th' accustom'd sight of death makes hard,
> Falls not the axe upon the humbled neck,
> But first begs pardon: will you sterner be
> Then he that dies and lives by bloody drops?

The Cambridge edition records nine monstrous substitutes for the phrase *dies and lives*. The simple fact is, that this phrase was a recognized *hysteron proteron;* and we are indebted to the Rev. W. R. Arrowsmith (*Notes and Queries*, 1st S. vii. 542) for a collection of early examples illustrating its use, which seem to have been entirely overlooked by all the previous editors and commentators. Mr. Halliwell, in his Folio Edition, supple-ments Mr. Arrowsmith's labours, but fails to recognize the fact that none of the examples adduced is precisely in point. That the phrase *to die and live* was formerly used for *to live and die*, is fairly established: but of the phrase *to die and live by a thing* not a single example has been adduced. Mr. Arrowsmith

tells us that *to die and live* means 'to subsist from the cradle to
the grave.' Shakespeare's executioner, then, must have been
initiated into his 'mystery' pretty early. But one of Mr.
Arrowsmith's examples is from a work now before us, *The
Pilgrimage of Kings and Princes:* at page 29 of which we
read, 'Behold how ready we are, how willingly the women of
Sparta will *die and live* with their husbands.' So that we are
gravely asked to believe that, according to this old writer, the
Spartan women were so precocious that they 'subsisted' with
their husbands 'from the cradle to the grave'! Hitherto, then,
no example in point has been discovered. But even if the
phrase *to die and live by a thing* be a Shakespearian idiasm,
its signification is as plain as the nose on one's face. It means
of course, *to make that thing a matter of life and death.* The
profession or calling of a man is that *by which he dies and lives,*
i. e., by which he lives, and failing which he dies.* In the face
of this simple exposition, emendation is a sheer impertinence.

3. Not infrequently we meet with a word or phrase
which, though sounding strange to us, was familiar enough in
Shakespeare's day, and may perhaps still retain a technical use.
Here are two examples in point. In 2 *Hen. IV.*, iv. 1, we find
Westmoreland thus sharply interrogating Archbishop Scroop,

> Wherefore doe you so ill translate your selfe,
> Out of the Speech of Peace, that beares such grace,
> Into the harsh and boystrous Tongue of Warre?
> Turning your Bookes to Graves, your Inke to Blood,
> Your Pennes to Launces, and your Tongue divine
> To a lowd Trumpet, and a Point of Warre.—Folio 1623.

* We owe this remark to our valued friend, Dr. Sebastian Evans.

For *Graves* Warburton would read *glaives*, and Steevens, *greaves*, and it is not easy to decide between them. But what can justify any tampering with the concluding expression, *a point of war* ? What can excuse such a conjecture as *report of war*, which stands in manuscript in the Perkins Folio, and in Mr. Collier's one-volume edition, or Mr. Singer's miserable gloss, *a bruit of war* ? Ignorance only; yet an ignorance which is hardly credible ; for not only was the expression *a point of war* as common as blackberries in Shakespeare's day, *but it is still in technical use.* It now means a drum-call, such as the ruffle-beat on parade, when the colours are unfurled. Steele in *The Tatler* used it in the same sense. In occurs frequently in Scott's novels (*e. g.*, *Waverley*, 1st ed., ii. 4; *Woodstock*, 1826, i. 21 & 142 ; and *The Bride of Lammermoor*, 1819, 247), where it always means a trumpet-call. It is also of very common occurrence in the old dramatists; and Macaulay has it in *Ivry*.

Then on the ground, while trumpets sound their loudest point of war, &c.

(See Staunton's illustrated edition of *Shakespeare*, i. 603.)

Our other example is from *Coriolanus*, v. 5, where Aufidius says of Coriolanus,

> [I] holpe to reape the Fame
> Which he did end all his ; and tooke some pride
> To do my selfe this wrong : (Folio 1623.)

There is not the faintest obscurity about this metaphor ; and nothing in this passage but the inflection 'holpe' is entirely obsolete, and that of course never stuck with anybody. The whole force of suspicion has fallen on the unoffending verb

end! Why, in the name of common sense ?   Aufidius says,
that he helped Coriolanus to reap the crop, that he endured
with him 'the burden and heat of the day,' but that Coriolanus
ended it, and made it all his own.*   Certainly no difficulty in
this phraseology would be presented to the mind of the rudest
midland farm-labourer.   We may still hear the farmers of
Worcestershire and Herefordshire employ that verb in a technical sense in speaking of their crops.

These points were very justly taken by the Rev. W. R. Arrowsmith in a sensible, but exceedingly scurrilous and ill-written
pamphlet entitled, *The Editor of Notes and Queries and his
Friend Mr. Singer.* (The title makes us wonder why some of the
shortest publications have the longest names : one of the Rev.
Joseph Hunter's, consisting of barely twenty-three pages, has a
title comprising sixty-eight words and twelve ciphers !) At p. 9,
Mr. Arrowsmith gives two newspaper-advertisements in which
occur the phrases, 'three excellent well-ended wheat-ricks,'
and 'a rick of well-ended hay.' We are almost ashamed of
insisting on anything so obvious : but where the suspected
phrase 'walks with his head in a crowd of poisonous flies,' it
is the duty of the critic at once to come to its aid ; and the
more innocent the phrase, the greater is that duty.   In this
case no less than five substitutes have been proposed for *end*

---

* Dr. Alexander Schmidt explains the passage thus : 'I helped to
gather the harvest which he consummated as his alone.   Perhaps [*end* is]
a technical phrase of harvest-work.' (*Shakespeare-Lexicon*, 1874.) It
certainly is so.   But to *reap* is not to *gather*.   *Ending* a crop is *gathering*
it.   A well-ended crop is one that is secured in good condition, or has
made a good end.'

or for *did end*, and three of these have been admitted into the text. Of these, the one which has found greatest favour is *ear* for *end*, which was proposed by Mr. Collier, and, with the transposition of *reap* and *ear*, was adopted by Mr. Singer. *To ear* is to plough, or till: so that Mr. Collier's reading makes Aufidius say he had his share of the harvest which Coriolanus had tilled for himself; (and even this sense is defective, since 'did ear' belongs to a later time than 'holpe;') but this is just the reversal of what Aufidius meant: for the gist of his complaint was that he had shared the toil with Coriolanus, and not the harvest. So the late Mr. W. N. Lettsom came to the rescue, and proposed (*Notes and Queries*, 1st S. vii. 378) the transposition of *ear* and *reap*. But matters were made no better by this: for Fame, as Mr. Arrowsmith promptly pointed out, is the crop; and though we *reap the crop*, we *ear* not the crop, but *the land*. It is noticeable that the clever and shrewd, but waspish critic of *Blackwood's Magazine* (Aug., Sept., and Oct., 1853), the merciless castigator of *Gnats and Queries* (as he designated Mr. W. J. Thoms' periodical), proposed the same transposition: so wonderfully do wits jump. What a satire on conjectural criticism is this little farce!

4. But what shall we say when a passage is entirely altered on the supposition that a word meant something which it never did mean, and does not mean at present? Yet this has happened to a passage in *Troilus and Cressida*, v. 2. When Troilus finds that Cressid has forsaken him for Diomed, he bursts into a passion of love and indignation, which is in Shakespeare's finest manner. He cries,

> This is, and is not *Cressid:*
> Within my soule there doth conduce a fight
> Of this strange nature, that a thing inseparate
> Divides more wider then the skie and earth:
> And yet the spacious bredth of this division
> Admits no Orifex for a point as subtle
> As *Ariachne's* broken woofe to enter: (Fo. 1623)

Shakespeare elsewhere employs very similar imagery: 'but I am not to say, it is the sea, for it is now the sky: betwixt the firmament and it you cannot thrust a bodkin's point,' *The Winter's Tale*, iii. 3; that is, though the sky and the sea are so widely divided, or separated, yet the sea mounts to such a height, that at times a point cannot be inserted between them. To this kind of equivocal division Troilus compares the separation between his heart and Cressid's. In reality the only question that can be rationally raised concerning this speech of Troilus' is as to the name Ariachne. That is the word of the Folio 1623. The quarto of 1609 has Ariachna, and the undated quarto has Ariathna. This variation is thought to favour the view, that the poet confounded the two names, Arachne and Ariadne, and possibly also the web of the former with the clew of the latter. Arachne was the spinner and weaver, and so subtle, *i. e.*, fine-spun (subtilis), was her woof, that when it was woven into the web, Minerva could not see how the web was made, and in a fit of jealousy and revenge tore it to pieces. If Shakespeare did confound the two fables, it was no more than his contemporaries did. Steevens quotes an example from Day's comedy of *Humour out of Breath*, 1608 (Steevens says 1607):

> And you in stead of these poore weeds in robes,
> Richer then that which Ariadne wroughte,
> Or Cytharaes aery-moving vestment.

Accordingly, we may see, if we like, Ariadne in both Ariathna and Ariachne:* but after all it may have been a custom of the time to write Ariachne for Arachne, if the metre required the additional syllable ; and we know that poets and dramatists enjoyed a very wide discretion in the presentation of proper names.

The point is of no moment. What it is of moment for us to see is that by Ariachne Shakespeare meant the spider into which Arachne was transformed, and which in Greek bears the same name ; and that the *woof* he meant was finer than was ever produced by human hand, viz., the woof of the spider's web—those delicate transverse filaments which cross the main radial threads or *warps*, and which are perhaps the nearest material approach to mathematical lines ! Thus has Shakespeare in one beautiful allusion wrapt up in two or three little words the whole story of Arachne's metamorphosis, the physical fact of the fineness of the woof-filaments of a spider's web,

---

* Milton made as great a mistake when he attributed to the eglantine the properties of the clematis. In *The Flower of Friendshippe*, Glomond Tylney, 1568 [8vo], we have, 'All the whole arbour above over our heades, &c., was * * * wreathed above with the sweete bryer or eglantine,' &c. In the *Faery Queen*, b. xi. c. 5, st. 29, Spenser describes an arbour,

> Through which the fragrant eglantine did spred
> His prickling armes, entrayled with roses red.

Yet Milton wrote

> Thro' the sweet briar or the vine,
> Or the *twisted* eglantine !

and an antithesis, effective in the highest degree, to the vastness of the yawning space between earth and heaven! For what orifice could be imagined more exquisitely minute than the needle's eye which would not admit the spider's woof to thread it? And this rich argosy has been wrecked by two transpositions.

The late Mr. Thomas Keightley, a gentlemen held in honour for his school histories, rather than for his unfortunate criticisms on Shakespeare, proposed in *Notes and Queries* (2nd S. ix. 358) what he considered an emendation of the passage we are considering; and subsequently had the temerity to incorporate this change with the text of a complete edition of Shakespeare's works. Observing that his great precursor Beckett had proposed to read,

> Subtile as Arachné's unbroken woof
> Admits no orifex for a point to enter,

whereby that monster had demonstrated to the world that he did not know the meaning of *woof*, Mr. Keightley undertook to amend the one line before adopting the other. The great gain, in his view, was that Ariachne had her eye put out, while the 'spacious breadth' was compared to Ariachne's *web!* So he read,

> And yet the spacious breadth of this division,
> As subtle as Arachne's broken woof,
> Admits no orifex for a point to enter.

Unfortunately, this is rank nonsense. How can a 'spacious breadth' be as subtle, or fine-spun, as a thread? Of course, it is easy to see that the whole farrago sprung from the one wretched blunder of taking a *woof* (which ever did and still does mean a thwart or cross-thread) to mean a *web.*

Again, we feel almost ashamed to have to resort to minute explanation of what every educated Englishman ought to know. In the operation of weaving, the threads which are stretched on the loom are called the *warp*, or *warps*, and the single thread which is carried through them by means of the shuttle is called the *woof;* and the two combined in a texture are called the *web.* This threefold distinction has been scrupulously observed by all accurate writers from very early times. One or two examples of the use of *woof*, from the literature of Shakespeare's day, may be acceptable, though supererogatory.

' *S. Hierome* would have *Paula* to handle woll, * * and learne to dress it, and to holde and occupie a rocke, [distaff] with a wooll basket in her lap, and turne the spindle, and drawe forth the thread with her own fingers. And *Demetrias* * * he bad have wooll in her hands, and her selfe either to spinne, to warpe, or else winde spindles in a case* for to throw *woofe* off, and to winde on clews the spinnings of others, and to order such as should be woven. * * * For should I call him a weaver that never learned to weave, nor to draw the *woffe*, nor to cast the shuttle, nor strike the web with the slaye.' Richard Hyrd's translation of L. Vives' *Instruction of a Christian Woman*, Book i. chap. 3, and Book ii. chap. 4.

* Probably *in a condition*, or *in order*, cf. *Tempest*, iii. 2. 'I am *in case* to justle a constable.'

5. In not a few cases the idiom of Shakespeare's day has been overlooked by every editor, and in some passages in his text the construction has been altered to make the unrecognised idiom square with modern usage. The most flagrant case that occurs to us, is that of 'the suppression of the relative as subject,' which, in a particular connection, has always created difficulty with the editors. Where the relative is suppressed before an auxiliary verb, the sense has always been too obvious to be overlooked: besides, in the case of its suppression before some tense of the verb *to be*, the practice still prevails in verse, and in epistolary prose. In *The Tempest*, v. 1, Prospero says to Alonzo and Sebastian,

> A solemne Ayre, and the best comforter,
> To an unsettled fancie, Cure thy braines
> (Now uselesse) boile within thy skull: there stand
> For you are Spell-stopt.   (Folio 1623)

Now in the first place, as two persons are addressed, and 'you' is the pronoun properly applied to them in the fourth line, it can hardly be doubted that the possessive pronoun 'thy' in the second and third lines is an error for *the*. Persons who have collated the old copies are familiar with this and similar misprints; the pronouns being under a singular fatality. Making this simple and necessary correction, and adopting modern spelling and punctuation, the passage will stand thus:

> A solemn air, and the best comforter
> To an unsettled fancy, cure the brains
> (Now useless) boil within the skull: &c.

To modern ears this construction sounds awkward: accordingly

Pope, having no sense of humour, altered 'boile' into *boil'd.*
It was a phrase of the time to say, that a man's brains boil or
are boiling, when he is mad or doting. In Chettle's play of
Hoffman, in the last scene, the hero, who, strange to relate,
manages to converse with his tormentors after he is crowned
with the traitor's red-hot crown, says,

> Ay so ;—boil on, thou foolish, idle brain,
> For giving entertainment to love's thoughts !

'Boiled brains' is in Shakespeare (*The Winter's Tale,* iii. 3),
but the phrase is humorous ; and otherwise inapplicable to the
men whom Prospero's spell had made frantic : whose brains
were *boiling* not *boiled.* The editors, having as little sense of
humour as Pope, have all adopted his abominable gloss. The
Rev. Wm. Harness, however, not long before his death privately
imparted to us his reading of the passage, which was on this
wise : a note of admiration being placed after 'fancy,' continue
thus :

> Sure thy brains
> (Now useless) boil within thy skull : &c.

which then seemed to us, and still seems, as imbecile as it is
unnecessary. It is as plain as the nose on one's face that the
above is an instance of 'the suppression of the relative as
subject' before the verb 'boil.' Paraphrase the passage thus :
'Let a solemn air—which is the best comforter to an unsettled
fancy—cure the brains [which], now useless, boil within the
skull.' 'An unsettled fancy' is a deranged mind, or 'incertain
thought' (as in *Measure for Measure*), 'settled' being Shakespeare's ordinary word for expressing soundness of mind ; and

'fancy' or phantasy, being equivalent to the faculty we call imagination.

With this example of the idiom in question compare the following:

> He loved me well * delivered it to me.—
>
> > > *Two Gentlemen of Verona*, iv. 4.
>
> I have a mind * presages me such thrift.—
>
> > > *Merchant of Venice*, i. 1.
>
> > But let your reason serve
> To make the truth appear, where it seems hid,
> And hide the false * seems true.—*Measure for Measure*, v. 1.
>
> Besides our nearness to the king in love
> Is near the hate of those * love not the king.—*Richard II.*, ii. 2.
>
> > What wreck discern you in me
> * Deserves your pity?—*Cymbeline*, i. 7.
>
> > Why am I bound
> By any generous bond to follow him
> * Follows his Taylor, haply so long untill
> The follow'd make pursuit?—*The Two Noble Kinsmen*, i. 2.
>
> > > Only you
> Of all the rest, are he * commands his love.—*Volpone*, i. 1.
>
> O then I find that I am bound,
> Upon a wheel * goes ever round.
>
> > > *Ariosto's Seven Planets*, &c. 1611.
> > > The Second Elegy (Appendix), p. 15.
>
> > Cast him off,
> Receive him not, let him endure the use
> Of their enforced kindnesse that must trust him,
> For meate and money, for apparrell, house,
> And every thing * belongs to that estate.—
>
> > > *All Fooles* (G. Chapman), i. 1.

I cast away a card now * makes me thinke
Of the deceased worthy King of Spaine.

Byrons Tragedie (G. Chapman), iv. 1.

The asterisk in each example shows where the relative (be it *which* or *who*) is to be understood.

6. Sometimes a word or idiotism presents no kind of difficulty, yet the passage is meaningless to modern readers, owing to the loss of some allusion of the time, which every one then understood in a moment. For example: in *Hamlet*, ii. 2, and iii. 2, we have three several allusions to the occasions of laughter during a theatrical performance: (1) The jests of the clown; (2) exaggerated or inadequate acting; (3) the *unseasonable* jests of the clown. As to the persons affected: in the first and third it is the thoughtless gigglers who are provoked to laughter: in the second, the 'unskilfull' who, seeing something out of keeping and absurd in the acting, are tickled to laughter, while the 'judicious' grieve over it. Hamlet welcomes the Clown, with the injunction that he shall 'speake no more then is set downe for him,' but reads the old player a lesson on the danger of exaggeration—which not only spoils the part, but distracts the thoughtless and moves them to unseasonable mirth. Now in the first allusion (ii. 2), Hamlet says, 'the clowne shall make those laugh whose lungs are tickled a the sere.' So the Folio 1623. For 'sere' Malone once conjectured *scene*. We doubtless ought to read with Mr. Staunton '*tickle* o' the sere.' Here is one example of *tickle* in this sense:

Ile give you my word; I have set her hart upon as *tickle* a pin as the needle of a Diall [Compass]; that will never let it rest, till it be in the right position. *The Widdowes Teares* (G. Chapman), ii. 2.

George Steevens offers an illustrative passage from *The Tempest*,
ii. 1, in case it should 'be of use to any future commentator.'
We thank him, and use it accordingly: it runs thus:

> I do well beleeve your Highnesse, and did it to minister occasion to
> these Gentlemen, who are of such sensible [sensitive] and nimble Lungs,
> that they always use to laugh at nothing.

So that 'whose lungs are tickle o' the sere,' should be of the
same meaning as, whose lungs are sensible and nimble—easily
made to explode in laughter. Yet Steevens failed to see it,
even with the material help of a couplet from a *Dialogue between
the Comen Secretary and Jelowsy, touchynge the Unstableness of
Harlottes.* (bl. l., n. d.)

> And wyll byde whysperynge in the eare,
> Thynk ye her tayle is not *light of the seare?*

Then came Douce, with a passage containing the very phrase
in question:

> Discovering the moods and humors of the vulgar sort (according to the
> touch of Affrike) to be so loose and *tickle of the seare.*—Howard's *Defensative
> against the Poyfon of supposed Prophecies.* 1620, fo. 31.

But Douce's eyes were held, and he could not see what was
under his nose. And when we think of it, this blindness of
Steevens, Douce, and their followers, to the drift (we say
nothing of the concrete sense) of the passage in *Hamlet*, is
passing wonderful. Here we have 'tickle o' the sere,' 'loose
and tickle of the seare,' and 'light of the seare;' and in the
two latter instances, the phrase must mean, *easily provoked to
the use of a natural function;* and we have besides Steevens'
parallel passage; so that it would appear impossible to resist

the logic—that ' tickle o' the sere,' applied to the lungs, must mean, *easily provoked to laughter.* Yet we have nothing but dogmatic assertions, that the phrase is an allusion to persons afflicted with the asthma, to whom laughter would be a painful operation : so that instead of ironical praise of the clown's poor jesting, the commentators understood Hamlet to be complimenting him on his power of extracting a laugh out of asthmatical lungs.* It was well that, at the eleventh hour, Dr. Brinsley Nicholson came to our rescue (*Notes and Queries,* 4th S., viii. 62), and at the twelfth, the Cambridge editors (Clarendon Press Series : *Hamlet,* p. 157); the latter quoting, for our eternal security, the following passage from Barret's *Theorike and Practike of Modern Warres,* 1598, p. 33 [35]: ' drawing down the *serre* with the other three fingers :'—after giving directions for holding the stock of the gun between the thumb and ~~three fingers~~ : so that the *serre, sere, seare,* or *scear,* is 'the catch in a gunlock, which keeps the hammer on half or full cock and is released by the trigger.' A gun which explodes with the least touch on the sere, was said to be *loose, light,* or *tickle of the sere;* hence the appropriateness of the

---

* ' Steevens' (say the Cambridge editors in this edition) 'explains it as signifying "those who are asthmatical, and to whom laughter is most uneasy. The real meaning is just the reverse." Steevens by uneasy, meant *unpleasant,* or even *painful;* and he expressly records that the baser sort, who were to be moved to laughter by the clown, might be those who have 'sensible and *nimble* lungs.' There is no opposition. An asthmatical person, to whom laughter may be painful, may also be one of those to whom laugher is too easy, and who 'always use to laugh at nothing.' Indeed, it would only be such an one, who would incur the consequences of an asthmatical cachinnation.

L

image to the penny-knaves' explosion of laughter on the lightest stimulus of the clown in a play.

Again, in *Love's Labour's Lost*, v. 1, Armado says to Holofernes,

> I do beseech thee, remember thy courtesy; I beseech thee, apparel thy head.

Neither Capell nor Malone understood it, and they therefore proposed emendations. The latter wished to insert *not :* 'remember not thy courtesy,' *i. e.*, pay no further regard to courtesy, but replace thy hat : as we should now say, ' do not stand on ceremony with me.' This was an absurd proposal, seeing that the phrase is frequent with the early dramatists; and in a curtalled form occurs in *Hamlet.* Yet Mr. Dyce (*Few Notes*, p. 56) adopted Malone's conjecture. But he returned to the old text at the instance of the writer, who gave in the *Illustrated London News* a complete defense of the old reading, from a manuscript note of Mr. Staunton's which will now be found in his edition of *Shakespeare*, vol. i. p. 83. Mr. Dyce on this occasion did not remember his courtesy: not only did he fail to acknowledge this service and assign to Mr. Staunton the credit of the restoration, but wrote contemptuously of the notes, of which this was one, evidently not perceiving that one and all were Mr. Staunton's. (See Dyce's *Shakespeare*, 1853.   Vol. i. p. ccxvi., and p. 581, note (13).)

But the origin of the expression, ' remember thy courtesy,' has never been given. It arose, we think, as follows : the courtesy was the temporary removal of the hat from the head, and that was finished as soon as the hat was replaced. If any

one from ill-breeding or from over-politeness stood uncovered
for a longer time than was necessary to perform the simple act
of courtesy, the person so saluted reminded him of the fact, that
the removal of the hat was a courtesy: and this was expressed
by the euphemism, 'Remember thy courtesy,' which thus implied, 'Complete your courtesy, and replace your hat.'

Here is another example in point. In *The Merry Wives of
Windsor*, ii. 3, the host says to Dr. Caius,

> I will bring thee where Mistris *Anne Page* is, at a Farm-house a
> Feasting : and thou shalt wooe her : Cride-game, said I well? (Fo. 1623.)

'Cried game' has been superseded in several modern
editions by 'Cried I aim,' a conjecture of Douce's. Various
other substitutes have been proposed. But why should the old
text be superseded? There can hardly be a doubt that under
the words 'Cried game,' if authentic, there lurks an allusion
of the time which has now to be hunted out. If 'cried game?'
be either *Is it cried game?* or *Cried I game?* we apprehend the
allusion is not far to seek. In hare-hunting, a person was employed and paid to find the hare, 'muzing on her meaze,' or,
as we say, in her form. He was called the hare-finder. When
he had found her, he first cried Soho! to betray the fact to
the pursuers ; he then proceeded to put her up, and 'give her
courser's law.' What, then, can 'Cried I game' mean but *Did
I cry game? Did I cry Soho?* In the play before us, the pursuit
was after Mistress Anne Page. She was the hare, and the host
undertook to betray her whereabouts to Dr. Caius in order that
he might urge his love-suit.

Again; there is a famous *crux* in *The Winter's Tale*, ii.
1, where four emendations have been proposed. Antigonus,
affirming the chastity of the queen against the jealous asper-
sions of Leontes, says—

            If it prove
    Shee's otherwise, Ile keep my Stables where
    I lodge my Wife, Ile goe in couples with her:
    Then when I feele, and see her, no farther trust her.   (Fo. 1623.)

With Rowe we may understand by 'then' the conjunction we
now write 'than'; *i. e.*, 'no farther than,' &c. Hanmer foolishly
read *my stable-stand*, for 'my stables'; Rann, *my stable;* Collier,
me stable (where *stable*, though made plural by the Cambridge
editors, is an adjective), and lastly the Cambridge editors, with
uncommon temerity, offer us the alternative of *my stabler*,
and *my stablers;* both of which we repudiate. Mr. Staunton,
adhering to the old text, attempted to fix upon it an interpretation, which is in the last degree far-fetched and offensive.
He seemed to think that there was but a step between Helen
and Semiramis.* For our part we look upon this passage as
the most instructive example, in all Shakespeare, of the danger
of tampering with the words of the old copies, in the absence
of that special knowledge which alone can give value to conjectural sagacity.

The verb to *keep* has various senses: some of these are, to

---

* Since neither Antigonus nor Leontes is a despicable villain like Iago,
it is a lame excuse for Mr. Staunton, that an image of the same degree
of grossness is put into the mouth of Iago. (*Othello*, i. 1.)

Zounds, sir, you are one of those, &c. .   . You'll have your daughters,
&c.

maintain; to *guard;* to *order;* to *continue* (or *remain*, v. n.): the first two senses are well illustrated by the following from *Nicholas Nickleby*, where, in reply to the remark " He *keeps* a manservant,' it is said, ' It's my opinion his manservant *keeps* him ;' *i. e.,* is his keeper. The second and third are here employed by Chapman (*Bussy D'Ambois*, i. 2).

> Our Roomes of State
> *Kept* like our stables : and though our Custome
> *Keepe* this assured confusion from our eyes, &c.

i. e., kept in a perpetual litter, and therefore ill-kept; and all this is guarded from inspection. In the passage which is the subject of our study, we agree with Mr. Staunton that ' keep ' is used in the sense of *guard:* but we go no further with him in his interpretation. The phrase to *keep one's stables* was a familiar phrase in Shakespeare's day; and meant to keep personal watch over one's wife's or one's mistress' chastity. We are sorry that it should be necessary to go into detail over so delicate an inquiry ; but as we intend to settle this matter for good and all, we will ask our readers, if they are qualmish on such matters, to omit the following paragraph.

In *All's Well that Ends Well* we have the following :

> I think I shall never have the blessing of God till I have issue a my body: for they say *barns* are blessings.

This fixes for us the sense of *barns, i. e.,* children. Now, in *Much Ado About Nothing*, iii. 4, we read:

> Yea, light o' love with your heels; then if your husband have *stables* enough, you'll look he shall lack no *barns*.

Of course there is a pun on *barns:* and there is a like pun on *stables*, which like *barns* had two meanings. When we know that *stables* was the condition precedent to *barns*, we have already pretty nearly determined its cant meaning. But a man's stable (or stables) may be kept by his wife, by himself, or by a third party, according to a notable custom in Italy: by the wife, if she be chaste; by the husband, if he be suspicious; by a third party, if she be unchaste and her husband be absent, unsuspicious, or indifferent. The passage in *The Winter's Tale* is an example of the second: of the other two cases the following will serve.

But for your wife that *keepes the stable* of your honour; Let her be lockt in a brazen towre, let *Argus* himselfe keepe her, yet can you never bee secure of your honour, for why? She can runne through all with her serpent nodle: besides you may hang a locke upon your horse, and so can you not upon your wife.*—Chapman's *All Fools*, act iv. sc. 2.

A young stripling . . . that can wait in a gentlewoman's chamber when his master is a mile off, *keep his stable* when 'tis empty, and his purse when 'tis full.—Green's *James the Fourth*.

(Quoted by Dyce, without understanding it, in his *Glossary*, ed. Sh., vol. ix. 1867, p. 233.)

Doubtless Rann's reading *stable*, would be strictly correct:

---

* This, however, was literally done by one Antonio Silvio, of Venice. The contrivance he employed used to be preserved in St. Mark's Palace. See *Ariosto's Seven Planets Governing Italie*, 1611, p. 61. A similar fetter used to be shewn at the Palais de Luxembourg, Paris. We observe a curious illustration in a letter from Laurence Sterne to his friend Hall (1764), reporting the progress of a love-suit with a Parisian lady: 'till at length I was within an ace of *setting up my hobby in her stable for good and all*,' i. e., making her his mistress. It was *her* stable: but had the clerical debauchee effected his purpose it would have been *his*.

but the plural may have been loosely used in the same sense as the singular.

7. Some expressions in the text, which were then, and still are, grammatical and significant, have been altered because their force is spent. They once had a sort of proverbial point, which is now wholly gone from them; hence they readily fall a prey to ingenious guessers. One instance will be sufficient to exemplify the class. In *As You Like It*, iii. 5, we read,

> Who might be your mother,
> That you insult, exult, and all at once,
> Over the wretched?

If emendation were wanted here, that of Theobald, adopted by Warburton, might be accepted, viz., *rail* for 'all.' Earlier in the same play we have (i. 1),

> Thou hast rail'd on thyself.

Compare also *Lear*, ii. 3,

> being down, insulted, rail'd
> And put upon, &c.

Yet the text is most certainly right. There is hardly a commoner phrase, more especially at the end of a verse, than *and all at once.* Compare *Henry V.*, i. 1,

> Nor never Hydra-headed wilfulness
> So soon did lose his seat, and all at once,
> As in this King.

The reader who desires to see other corroborative instances from writers of the time may consult Mr. Staunton's illustrated edition of *Shakespeare*, vol. ii. p. 65. In this case the Cambridge editors give us a truly wonderful collection of conjectures, one of which is Hanmer's *domineer!* and that feat of dulness is capped by another, which consists of three French words!

8. But more curious still, there are passages which have occasioned a considerable amount of discussion, and have even received emendation, not on account of anything difficult or corrupt in the construction, but simply because no one among the swarm of critics had seized the central or leading notion of the speaker. The two following, which are selected from many cases in point occurring in the same play, may serve as samples of the class. In *As You Like It*, iii. 2, Rosalind plies Celia with some questions respecting Orlando: and having reminded her friend, that, though she (Rosalind) is caparisoned like a man, she has a woman's curiosity, adds,

> One inch of delay more, is a South-sea of discoverie. I pre'thee tell me who it is quickly, and speak apace: I would thou couldst stammer, &c. Is he of God's making? What manner of man? Is his head worth a hat? or is his chin worth a beard? (Fo. 1623.)

The unfortunate association of 'South-sea' with a supposed voyage of 'discoverie' affords perhaps some explanation of the fact that the central or leading notion has always been missed. Here we have a tale of questions—*coup sur coup*—falling as thick as hail upon the devoted Celia. See how many things she is called upon to *discover;* and then say whether she has not incurred a laborious and vexatious duty by her *delay* in answering the first question. How plain it is that her *inch* of delay has cast her upon a *South Sea*—a vast and unexplored ocean—of discovery. The more Celia delays her revelation as to who the man is, the more she will have to reveal about him. Why? Because Rosalind fills up the delay (increases it, in fact) with fresh interrogatories, whereby Celia becomes lost in a South Sea of questions.

There is surely some fatality about this play, for we observe several other passages in it, which, without more than the shadow of a pretence, have been altered in every, or almost every, edition. For instance, in ii. 6, Jaques says:

> Hee, that a Foole doth very wisely hit,
> Doth very foolishly, although he smart
> Seeme senselesse of the bob. If not,
> The Wise-man's folly is anathomiz'd
> Even by the squandering glances of the foole.
>
> (Fo. 1623.)

Theobald, being conscious of a hitch in the sense, proposed 'Not to seem senseless' for 'Seeme senselesse.' In this lead he has been usually followed, even by the Cambridge editors. Had they seized the central notion of the passage, they would not have done so. Why does a fool do *wisely* in hitting a wise man? Because, through the vantage of his folly, he puts the wise man 'in a strait betwixt two,' to put up with the smart of the bob, without dissembling, and the consequential awkwardness of having to do so—which makes him feel foolish enough —or, to put up with the smart, *and dissemble it*, which entails the secondary awkwardness of the dissimulation—which makes him feel still more foolish. Taking the former alternative, *i. e.*, 'If not' ('If *he do* not') his 'folly is anatomized even by the squandering glances of the fool'; taking the latter alternative,

M

he makes a fool of himself in the eyes of almost everybody
else.   So the fool gets the advantage both ways.   There is a
passage in a paper of De Quincey's called 'Literary Novitiate,'
published in vol. i. of *Literary Reminiscences* (Ticknor and
Field's edition), which has a special bearing on the above
passage.   At page 25 we read, 'Awkwardness at the least —
and too probably, as a consequence of *that*, affectation and
conceit — follow hard upon the consciousness of special notice
or admiration.   The very attempt to disguise embarrassment
too often issues in a secondary and more marked embarrassment.'   How plain, then, is the sense of the passage we are
considering.   Jaques asks for 'the motley,' in order that he
may have a fool's privilege of making a fool of every wise man.
In *Othello*, i. 3, is a passage which, with a very different bearing,
may serve to illustrate this.

> What cannot be preserved when fortune takes,
> Patience her injury a mockery makes.
> The robb'd that smiles, steals something from the thief;
> He robs himself, that spends a bootless grief.

Observing that the line,

> Seeme senselesse of the bob.   If not,

is too short, we think it probable that the words *he do* originally
formed part of it.   Be that as it may, 'If not' must mean 'If
he do not.'   Perhaps, 'Very foolishly' should be in a paren-
thesis; and 'very wisely' might be so also.

9.   A strictly methodical discussion of classes of readings,
even if it were practicable, would not present any very great

advantage: so we have not attempted it. We will now proceed
to consider two of the cases in which Shakespeare has metaphorically employed the image of *a sea:* viz., 'a sea of wax,'
and 'a sea of troubles.'

The pedantic poet in *Timon of Athens*, i. 1, addresses the
painter in the following tumid and bombastic terms:

> You see this confluence, this great flood of visitors.
> I have in this rough work shaped out a man [*shewing his manuscript*]
> Whom this beneath world both embrace and hug
> With amplest entertainment: my free drift
> Halts not particularly, but moves itself
> In a wide sea of wax: no levell'd malice
> Infects one comma of the course I hold;
> But flies an eagle's flight, bold and forth on,
> Leaving no tract behind.

In this passage, 'my free drift' and 'a wide sea of wax' are
contrasted with the notion of 'halting particularly' and 'levell'd
malice.' In other words, the poet is contrasting generality with
particularity. The visitors who throng the presence-chamber of
Lord Timon are compared by the poet to a sea, or arm of the
sea, when the tide is rising, and are therefore designated a
'confluence' and a 'great flood.' Timon is said to be em-
braced 'with amplest entertainment' by this flood; and the
poet, disclaiming particular personal censure, asserts, in a metaphor probably derived from Archery, that 'no levell'd malice
infects one comma,' *i. e.*, not a single clause, in his poem. It
is the antecedent sentence which contains the stumbling-block.
What is the meaning of 'a wide sea of wax?' Every one
knows that the verb *to wax* means, to grow; and the old English

writers employ it indifferently of increase or decrease; a thing,
with them, may wax greater or smaller, stronger or weaker. *To
wax* was to change condition simply.   But more strictly it was
and is still used in opposition to *wane*. If anything changes
its condition, it either waxes or wanes. In this restricted sense
Shakespeare in several places uses the verb *to wax* of the sea.

> Who marks the waxing sea grow wave by wave.—
> *Titus Andronicus*, iii. 1.

> His pupil-age
> Man-enter'd thus, he waxed like a sea.—*Coriolanus*, ii. 1.

The older editors and commentators seem not to have had the
faintest suspicion of the meaning of the expression, 'a wide
sea of wax.' Hanmer and Steevens explain it as an allusion
to the Roman and early English practice of writing with a style
on tablets coated with wax, so that the poet in *Timon* must be
supposed literally to have 'shaped out' his man in wax, almost
as much so as if he had modelled him. All the editors have
followed this lead. Mr. Dyce to the last was confirmed in this
interpretation; but Mr. Staunton, who had once accepted it,
was at length conducted to the extraordinary conclusion, that
'wax' was a press-error for *tax !* Besides this, the only emendation attempted is Mr. Collier's *verse*. Very strange indeed is
all this speculation, in the face of the certain fact, that the
substantive, *wax*, occurs elsewhere in Shakespeare in an allied
sense.

> *Chief Justice.* What ! you are as a candle, the better part burnt out.
> *Falstaff.* A wassail candle, my lord; all tallow: if I did say of wax,
> my growth would approve the truth.—2 *Henry IV.*, i. 2.

It is all very well to say that this is a quibble or pun: it is so: but such a pun would be insufferable—not to say impossible— unless there were a substantive *wax*, meaning growth, on which to make the pun. It is, indeed, open to question whether *wax* be used in this sense, in the proverbial phrase 'a man of wax,' which occurs in *Romeo and Juliet*, i. 3.* 'A wide sea of wax' seems to be merely an affected and pedantic mode of indicating a sea that widens with the flood.

In *Hamlet*, iii. i, we read:

> Whether 'tis nobler in the mind to suffer
> The slings and arrows of outrageous fortune,
> Or to take arms against a sea of troubles,
> And by opposing end them:

Hamlet's question implies an option, either to endure his troubles, or to end them, even at the cost of his life. If 'a sea of troubles' be taken to mean *a troublous sea* (somewhat as in

---

* I formerly accepted Mr. Brae's view, that in Ben Jonson's posthumous fragment *The Fall of Mortimer*, the word *waxe* had the sense of personal aggrandisement: but I am now convinced that Mr. Dyce was quite right in referring the word in question to the waxen seal attached to the Earl's patent of nobility. Evidently Mortimer is noting the *outward* insignia of his rank—viz., his 'crownet,' his 'robes,' and the Great Seal, which *he bore in his hand*. This last is a point overlooked by Mr. Dyce. Mr. Brae, who has privately retracted his interpretation, refers me to *Nobilitas Politica vel Civilis*, by Robert Glover, Somerset Herald: edited in 1608 by his nephew Thomas Milles. He tells us that an Earl 'bore a patent with the Great Seal pendent by Cord and Tassel.' Mr. Brae seems to have been misled by the two lines which follow 'crownet, robes, and waxe,' in Jonson's play, in which he saw a possible allusion to the poet's speech in *Timon*.

> There is a fate that flies with towering spirits
> Home to the mark, and never checks at Conscience.

But the metaphor is taken from hawking.

the passage we have just considered 'a sea of wax' means *a
waxing sea*, or a sea rising at flood tide), the phrase 'to take arms
against a sea of troubles' expresses as futile a feat as 'to wound
the still-closing waters.' Would Shakespeare have put such a
catachresis into the mouth of the philosophical Hamlet? The
doubt thus engendered has manifested itself, as usual, in a
plentiful crop of emendations, which in this case are all ingenious, with the exception of one proposed by the late Mr.
Samuel Bailey. By far the best is Mr. A. E. Brae's conjecture
of *assay* for 'a sea.' In the presence of that we think it impertinent to name its rivals. It is not only singularly clever,
but it gives a sense, force, and dignity to the passage, which,
thus emended, is in Shakespeare's best manner. But this is
not enough.

In the first place let us clearly realize the fact, that the
metaphor, *a sea of troubles, sorrows, griefs, dangers*, &c., is as
old as the hills, and is found in all languages: and it is admirably expressive of the two attributes of those sorrows that
come 'in battalions,' their multiplicity, and their power to overwhelm. Accordingly no defense or illustration of the figure is
needed. Moreover it has been contended by many critics, as
Johnson, Malone, Warburton (in his second thoughts), Caldecott,
De Quincey, and Staunton, that the want of consistency or
integrity in this metaphor is no argument against Shakespeare
having written the passage as it stands. Caldecott (*Specimen of
a New Edition of Shakespeare*, 1819, p. 65) puts it thus: ' He
uses it [the metaphor] himself everywhere and in every form:
and the integrity of his metaphor is that which by him is of

all things the least thought of.' In support of this assertion
Caldecott refers to three passages in Shakespeare, not one of
which bears it out. The fact is, that Shakespeare employs *sea*
figuratively eight times: viz., *Timon of Athens*, i. 1, 'sea of wax';
and iv. 2, 'sea of air': *Pericles*, v. 1, 'sea of joys': *Henry VIII.*,
iii. 2, 'sea of glory'; and ii. 4, 'sea of conscience': 1 *Henry VI.*,
iv. 7, 'sea of blood': *Lucrece*, st. 158, 'sea of care'; and the
instance in question. In every case, except the last which is on
its trial, the integrity of the metaphor is sufficiently preserved.
That, however, in *Timon of Athens*, iv. 2, has been thought
questionable; and Mr. Richard Garnett (*Athenæum*, October
15, 1859), after quoting the lines,

> Leak'd is our bark,
> And we, poor mates, stand on the dying-deck,
> Hearing the surges threat; we must all part
> Into *this sea of air*,

remarks—'I, for one, can neither understand the phrase in italics,
nor correct it.' Without asserting that these lines were written
by Shakespeare, we may very readily illustrate their meaning.
' Part,' of course, is *depart;* * and the 'sea of air' is that into
which the soul, freighting his wrecked bark, the body, must at
length take its flight. Compare with the above, the following
from Drayton's *Battle of Agincourt:*

> Now where both armies got upon that ground,
> As on a stage, where they their strengths must try,
> Whence *from the width of many a gaping wound*
> *There's many a soul into the air must fly.*

---

* The converse is the case with an expression in the Marriage Service;
so in Green's *Groatsworth of Wit:* 'but I am yours till death us depart.'

As to Shakespeare's metaphor in the passage under con-
sideration, 'a sea of troubles,' it occurs once in the *Faerie
Queen* (Book VI. c. ix. st. 31); and the sea is otherwise employed metaphorically by Spenser in many places (see the
Faerie Queen, Book I. c. xii. st. 14: Book III. c. iv. st. 8, &c.),
but not once does he do violence to the metaphor. It is also
frequently found in prose works of the time. In Sir Richard
Morysine's translation of L. Vives' *Introduction to Wysedom*,
Book IV., we have 'sea of evils'; and in Andrew Kingsmyll's
Comforts in Afflictions (fol. 6) we have 'seas of sorrows': and
in both cases is the integrity of the metaphor preserved. Are
we, then, to believe that Shakespeare departed from this conscientious custom in one passage, where *a sea* is not an improbable misprint for *assay?*

We are thus presented with the horns of a dilemma: viz., on
the one hand the imputation of a lame metaphor to Shakespeare's
most philoscphic character, and on the other, a conjectural
emendation. Now it seems to us that there is a way out of
this dilemma—a middle course which has hitherto escaped the
notice of the critics. One consideration of the highest importance has been entirely ignored. When Hamlet talked of
ending his sea of troubles, or, as he afterwards describes it,
shuffling off his mortal coil,* he had a covert consciousness, a

---

* Shakespeare represents the human body under various figures: a
coil: a *case*: a *frame*: a *machine*: a *vesture*: a *heft*: a *motion* or puppet:
&c. It has been contended that in Hamlet's speech, the 'mortal coil' is
the coil, *i. e.*, trouble or turmoil, incident to man's mortal state: but the
analogies are too strong in favour of the 'mortal coil' being what Fletcher
calls the 'case of flesh.' (*Bonduca*, iv. 1.)

conscience, in fact, which stayed the hand he would have raised against his own life; viz., that this so-called ending and shuffling off, was a mere delusion, just as much so as repelling the advancing waves of the sea with shield and spear. Is not the metaphor, then, sound and whole? If there be an incongruity in the notion of taking arms, offensively or defensively, against the sea, is there not just as great an incongruity in using 'a bare bodkin' against the soul—the immortal part, which (as Raleigh has it) 'no stab can kill'? But, in fact, that seeming incongruity is defensible, quite apart from the metaphor. The late Mr. Samuel Bailey, in his discussion of the passage in question, has the following remark: 'The objection is not to the metaphorical designation *a sea of troubles*, [—who ever said it was?] but to the figurative absurdity implied in "taking up arms against a sea of troubles," or indeed against any other sea, literal or imaginary. I question whether any instance is to be found of such a fight in the whole compass of English Literature.' (*The Received Text of Shakespeare*, p. 39.) Why restrict the search to English Literature? But the instance we have in view is to be found in various literatures. In Ritson's *Memoirs of the Celts* (p. 118) occurs the following passage, which is a translation of one in Ælian :

'Of all men I hear that the Celts are most ready to undergo dangers. * * * So base, indeed, do they consider it to fly, that frequently they will not escape out of houses tumbling down and falling in upon them, nor even out of those burning, though themselves are ready to be

N

caught by the fire. Many, also, oppose the overwhelming
sea : there are some, likewise, who taking arms rush
upon the waves, and sustain their attack, extending their
naked swords and spears, in like manner as if they were
able to terrify or wound them.'

The same tradition is referred to by Aristotle in his Eudemian
Ethics, iii. 1 :

οἶον οἱ Κελτοὶ πρὸς τὰ κύματα ὅπλα ἀπαντῶσι λαβόντες.

See also Arist. Nich. Eth. iii. 7.

We think, then, Hamlet's soliloquy might be fairly paraphrased
thus :

' To exist: or to cease to exist: that is the question for me
to decide.   Whether it is the nobler part to endure the
outrages of fortune, and to dare the surrounding sea of
troubles ; or to imitate the fabled feats of the Celts, and
" taking arms to rush upon the waves."   Doubtless it is
far nobler to endure unshaken ; and is it not also more
prudent ? For, it seems probable, that the attempt to end
our troubles by self-destruction would be as futile as that
of the Celts to assail the ocean ; and that after death
itself we should find ourselves overwhelmed by evils of
which we know nothing, and which therefore, for aught
we know, may be greater than those from which we should
have escaped.   Thus does conscience make cowards of
us all.'

All things considered, then, in the case before us, we elect to adhere to the received text, and refuse to allow even the most admirable of emendations to allure us from our allegiance to a consistent metaphor which has all the external evidences of authenticity.

While on this famous soliloquy, we may as well note that

> The undiscovered country from whose bourn
> No traveller returns

is the allegorical country of the Meropes, well known to every reader in Shakespeare's day. In the fifth discourse of the Spanish Mandevile (London, 1600, p. 126), Bernardo, one of the interlocutors, says,

'That which I will tell you is out of Theopompus, alleaged by Ælianus in his book *De varia Historia.* [It is in Æl. Var. Hist. iii. 18.] This Sylenus * * * * in one communication that hee had with King Mydas, discoursed unto him, that out of this Land or world in which wee live * * * * there is another Land so great that it is infinite and without measure * * * * and the men which dwell therein are twise so great as we are, and their life twise as long * * * *. There were in other provinces thereof certain people called Meropes, who inhabited many and great Citties, within the bounds of whose Country there was a place called Anostum, which word signifieth, a place whence there is no returne: this Country, saith he, is not cleare and light, neither yet altogether darke, but between both, through the same

runne two Rivers, the one of delight, the other of griefe,'
&c.*

It is noteworthy, too, that 'the undiscovered country' is not
mentioned in the 4to, 1603. Shakespeare may have read this
passage in Ælian between 1602 and 1604, in which latter year
the first enlarged *Hamlet* was published, containing the allusion
to Anostum.

10. Some of the obscurities in Shakespeare's text arise
from the consilience of two sources of perplexity. Here is one
example, in which a word employed in an obsolete sense forms
part of a phrase which is itself of peculiar construction. In
Hamlet, i. 4, Horatio tries to dissuade *Hamlet* from accompanying
the ghost, lest it should

> assume some other horrible form,
> Which might deprive your sovereignty of reason,
> And draw you into madness.

The verb *to deprive* is at present used with the same construction as *bereave* or *rob;* but in Shakespeare it corresponds to our
ablate. Thus in *Lucrece,* st. clxx. :

> 'Tis honour to deprive dishonour'd life.

And again in st. ccli. :

> That life was mine which thou hast here depriv'd.

But the passage from *Hamlet* contains yet another source of
perplexity, viz., to 'deprive your *sovereignty of reason,*' *i. e.*, to

* For these two illustrations from Ælian we are indebted to our friend
Dr. Sebastian Evans : who from the passage in *Hamlet* would omit the
pronoun after 'end,' understanding by that verb *die.*

deprive the sovereignty of your reason; or, as we should more naturally say, to deprive your reason of its sovereignty:* in view of which the Rev. Joseph Hunter *(Few Words)* proposed to transpose 'your' and 'of.' In defense of the original text, take the following from a letter of Sir Thomas Dale, 1616 (the year of Shakespeare's death). He calls Virginia 'one of the goodliest and richest kingdoms in the world, which being inhabited by the king's subjects, will put such a bit into our ancient enemy's mouth as will curb *his hautiness of monarchy.*'

11. Occasionally it is the figurative language of the text which throws the critic on a false scent, and thus leads him to look for a corruption where there is none. The best example which we can call to mind is a passage in *Much Ado About Nothing*, iv. 1. Leonato, learning that Hero has fainted under the shock of her disgrace, cries,

> Do not live, Hero, do not ope thine eyes:
> For, did I think thou wouldst not quickly die,
> Thought I thy spirits were stronger than thy shames,
> Myself would on the rearward of reproaches
> Strike at thy life.

This is the reading of the quarto, which has the spelling *rereward.* The military metaphor has perplexed the critics.

---

* It is purely an accident that the object of 'deprive' is expressed by two substantives connected by *of*, suggesting to the modern reader the construction here given. A learned friend suggests that in some possible poem, entitled (say) 'The Battle of the High and the Low,' the following might occur:

> To make an application to the bishop,
> Who might deprive the rector of the parish,
> And turn him out of office.

The war is between Hero's spirits and her shames or reproaches. The latter have, in the onset, assailed her, and she lies insensible from their violence.   Then says Leonato, 'if owing to the sustaining power of her spirits, her reproaches fail to kill her, I will come, as a reserve, in their rear, and I will slay her myself.' Not perceiving the integrity of the metaphor, for which 'rearward' (the opposite of *voyward, vayward,* or *vanguard*) is absolutely required, Mr. A. E. Brae, this time most infelicitously, proposed to read *reword* for the reading of the folio, 'reward.' This reading would greatly weaken the passage ; for as it stands, the very deficiency of the reproaches (which are enough to prostrate, but not to kill her) is the reason for Leonato's interference: whereas Mr. Brae's reading seems to make him say, that if that deficiency were abated, if their power were recruited, he would then interpose to do a work of supererogation.   But this reading distinguishes between Hero's *shames* and her *reproaches,* which are evidently one and the same. If, then, the text were faulty, Mr. Brae's reading would be no cure, but, if anything, make matters worse.   The objection to *reward,* taken in the old sense of *regard,* or to *reword,* on the ground of prosody, would be untenable.   *Reward* and *reword* might be indifferently iambuses or trochees.   *Relapse, severe, supreme,* and *secure* (Shakespeare), *reflect* (Fletcher), *regret* (Drant), *revere* (May), and *recluse* (Donne), are all occasionally used as trochees.   The real objection to *reward* is, that the sense of *regard* was already obsolete when Shakespeare wrote; that to *reword* is, that it makes Leonato's declaration inconsistent with itself and violates the integrity of the metaphor, or else it degrades Hero's reproaches (her shames, in fact) into verbal accusations ('upon the repetition of these charges' is Mr. Brae's paraphrase): to both alike, that the relative text presents no difficulty to the reader who understands the military figure which it involves, and therefore no footing for the conjectural critic. We have, in fact, the same metaphor, in Shakespeare's 90th Sonnet, which in one version has also suffered emendation ('woe' being altered into *foe*):

> Oh! do not, when my heart hath scap'd this sorrow
> *Come in the rearward of a conquer'd woe;*
> Give not a windy night a rainy morrow,
> To linger out a purpos'd overthrow.
> If thou wilt leave me, do not leave me last,
> When other petty griefs have done their spite,
> *But in the onset come;* so shall I taste
> At first the very worst of Fortune's might; &c.

We will give one more example of the same fatality. Shakespeare's figurative use of the word *stain*, whether substantive or verb, is various. The primary notion is that of giving to something a colour from without; this may be a stain of foulness or otherwise, and *stain* may thus mean *pollute, pollution;* or somewhat more generally, *dishonour;* otherwise, *dye, indue* (verb, in Shakespeare's peculiar sense), and therefore *subdue* (verb), *i. e.,* to a particular attribute or quality; and again, *infect, infection,* and finally *compromise.* In another view the substantive *stain* may signify the reverse of *foil,* as in *Venus and Adonis,* st. *Y,* 'stain to all nymphs,' *i. e.,* casting their charms into the *shade* by comparison with those of V̶e̶n̶u̶s̶. The passage we have in view, in making these remarks, is in *Antony and*

Cleopatra, iii. 4. Antony complains to Octavia that her brother
has gone to war against Pompey without reason, and without
his (Anthony's) concurrence; that he has given him (Antony)
'narrow measure' in speaking of him. This touches his honour,
and he therefore declares that while his wife goes, as reconciler,
between the two triumvirs, he will give Cæsar a strong motive
for making overtures of friendship. He says,

> The mean time, lady,
> I'll raise the preparation of a war
> Shall *stain* your brother.

The metaphor, which once seized can never occasion the least
perplexity, has misled the critics, who have accordingly attempted
to remedy a seeming imperfection by treating 'stain' as a misprint. Theobald reads *strain;* Boswell proposed *stay*, which
Mr. J. P. Collier and Mr. A. Dyce adopted, the latter complimenting his two predecessors on having perceived 'what was
the true remedy (Dyce's ed. 1867, vol. vii, p. 612).' Rann has
'*stain* for *sustain*. Jackson proposed *stun;* and the Cambridge
Edition records an anonymous conjecture, *slack!* Certainly,
had *strain* been in the old text we should have been well satisfied with it. But while regarding that as *facile princeps* among
the proposed substitutes, we hold it to be quite inferior to the
word of the folio. *Compromise* would be a dilution of *stain*, in
the sense we believe Shakespeare to have intended. Antony's
preparation was designed to effect a total change in Cæsar's
purposes and plans, in fact to indue and subdue him to the
quality of Antony's mind—possibly even to overshadow Cæsar,
and impress him with the weight of Antony's personal character.

As it seems to us, we are losers by adopting any of the proposed substitutes. Our bard eschewed, for the most part, weak generalities, and, though his word *stain* have a considerable range of meaning, it is preserved from vagueness by its anchorage in the world of sense.

12. Some passages present a cluster of difficulties — so many, in fact, that it cannot be supposed that mere textual corruption can have originated them all. Two salient examples occur respectively in *Measure for Measure*, iii. 1, and *Cymbeline*, v. 4; both relating to death. The former runs thus:

> I, but to die, and go we know not where,
> To lie in cold obstruction, and to rot,
> This sensible warm motion, to become
> A kneaded clod; And the delighted spirit
> To bath in fierie floods, or to recide
> In thrilling Region of thicke-ribbed Ice,
> To be imprison'd in the viewlesse windes
> And blowne with restlesse violence round about
> The pendant world: or to be worse then worst
> Of those, that lawlesse and incertaine thought,
> Imagine howling, 'tis too horrible. (Folio 1623.)

The opening of this passage was specially selected by Mr. J. M. D. Meiklejohn, in a paper read to the *College of Preceptors*, as an illustration of his assertion, that the practice of calling upon a student to write a paraphrase of poetry is useless and absurd : here he pronounced a paraphrase to be impossible. Now a paraphrase is only impossible through some inherent obscurity in the text to be expounded : and surely the more difficult a passage is, the more useful is the paraphrase. To us

o

it appears plain that the practice of calling for a paraphrase is in the highest degree commendable: for it is the only means by which the teacher can discover how far the pupil understands the passage which forms the subject of his study.　Not that a paraphrase can by any means convey the whole sense of the original: no paraphrase was ever intended to do that: but it can convey, by analysis and qualification, the greater part of that sense; and surely 'half a loaf is better than no bread.' We do not 'halt particularly' to expound the meaning of 'cold obstruction' or 'delighted spirit:' we would rather call attention to Shakespeare's use of the abstract substantive, as 'Region' and 'thought.'　Dyce's first edition thus remarks upon the former word: 'The folio has "Region": but the plural is positively required here on account of "*floods*" in the preceding and "*winds*" in the following line.'　And for the latter he reads, after all the editors, save those of Oxford and Cambridge, '*thoughts.*'　That note, if it mean anything, means that Shakespeare employed *Region* [*s*] in the concrete, and in the modern and ordinary sense: and we have no doubt that Dyce adopted the plural *thoughts* as the nominative to 'imagine.'　On the contrary we contend that 'Region' is used as an abstract, and in the radical sense; and that it means *restricted place*, or *confinement :* * also, that 'thought' is used as an abstract, and that it is the objective governed by 'imagine.'　The adjective 'incer-

---

* So Carlyle appears to have understood it : for in his *Heroes and Hero-worship*, 1842, Lect. iii. p. 135, he quotes the passage à *propos* of Dante's 'soft etherial soul, looking out so stern, implacable, grim-trenchant, as from *imprisonment of thick-ribbed ice!*' as expressed in Giotto's portrait. He is perhaps also glancing at *L'Inferno*, Canto xxxiv.

tain' is employed in a specialised sense, like the Latin *incertus:* *certain* like *certus,* is elsewhere used by Shakespeare as opposed to flawed or crazed: *e. g.,* in *A Midsummer Night's Dream,* i. 1, Demetrius says,

> Relent, sweet Hermia; And Lysander yield
> Thy *crazed* title to my *certain* right;

and again in ii. 2,

> That the *rude* sea grew *civil* at her song,
> And *certain* stars shot *madly* from their spheres, &c.

In fact, *certain* and *incertain* are synonyms for *settled* and *un-settled,* respectively. (See 'so muddy, so unsettled,' and 'settled senses,' *Winter's Tale,* i. 2 and v. 3; and 'unsettled fancy,' *Tempest,* v. 1.) Accordingly, as we read the passage, the last three lines may be paraphrased thus:

> 'or to be in an infinitely worse case than those who body forth—or render objective—their own lawless and distracted mind.'

The pendant from *Cymbeline,* v. 4, is as follows:

> Most welcome bondage! For thou art a way,
> I think, to liberty. Yet am I better
> Than one that's sick o' the gout, since he had rather
> Groan so in perpetuity, than be cured
> By the sure physician, Death; who is the key
> To unbar these locks. My conscience! thou art fettered
> More than my shanks and wrists. You good gods give me
> The penitent instrument to pick that bolt,
> Then free for ever! Is't enough I'm sorry?
> So children temporal fathers do appease:

> Gods are more full of mercy. Must I repent?
> I cannot do it better than in gyves
> Desir'd more than constrain'd. To satisfy,
> (If of my freedom 'tis the main part) take
> No stricter render of me than my all.
> I know you are more clement than viled men,
> Who of their broken debtors take a third,
> A sixth, a tenth, letting them thrive again
> On their abatement; that's not my desire:
> For Imogen's dear life take mine; and though
> 'Tis not so dear, yet 'tis a life: you coin'd it.
> 'Tween man and man they weigh not every stamp;
> Though light, take pieces for the figure's sake;
> You rather, mine being yours: and so, Great Powers,
> If you will take this audit, take this life,
> And cancel these cold bonds.

Of the passage from 'Must I repent,' down to 'my all,' Mr. Staunton writes, 'It is, we fear, hopelessly incurable.' To which we can only answer, that we see in it no corruption whatever! Difficulty there is, but none that does not disappear in the simple process of elucidation. In our judgment the entire passage is one of those in which the bard displays at once his wealth of knowledge and his fertility of language. Its terseness, along with a certain technical and figurative use of words, has misled all the critics: and, as the result of their industry, we have nothing but laboured misprision and wanton innovation. In Shakespeare-criticism we learn to be grateful for negative virtues: and we are really thankful that Mr. Staunton, warned by the example of Hanmer, presents the passage intact and entire, and spares us the pain of conjectural corruption. Posthumus rejoices in his bodily thraldom, because its issue will be death, which will set him free: certainly from bodily bondage, and possibly from spiritual bondage — the worse of the twain. So he prays for 'the penitent instrument to pick *that* bolt,' the bolt which fetters his conscience worse than the cold gyves constrain his shanks and wrists: that is, for the means of a repentance which may be efficacious for pardon and absolution. He then enters into these means in detail, following the order of the old Churchmen: viz., sorrow for sin, or *attrition:* 'Is't enough I am sorry?' &c.: then penance, which was held to convert attrition into *contrition:* 'Must I repent?' &c.: then *satisfaction* for the wrong done. As to this last he says, if the main condition of his spiritual freedom be that ('To satisfy'), let not the gods *with that object* require a stricter render than his all—his life. These are the three parts of absolution. The third he expands in the last clause. He owns that his debt exceeds his all. He says, in effect,

> 'Do not call me to a stricter account than the forfeiture of my all *towards* payment. Take my all, and give me a receipt, not on account, but in full of all demands. Earthly creditors take of their debtors a fraction of their debt and less than their all, "letting them thrive again on their abatement": but I do not desire that indulgence of your clemency. Take life for life—my all: and though it is not worth so much as Imogen's, yet 'tis a life, and of the same divine origin: a coin from the same mint. Between man and man light pieces are current for the

sake of the figure stamped upon them: so much the rather should the gods take my life, which is in their own image, though it is not so dear, or precious, as Imogen's.'*

The old writers compared the hindrances of the body to gyves: so Walkington in *The Optick Glasse of Humors*, 1607 (fo. 11), 'Our bodies were the prisons and bridewils of our soules, wherein they lay manicled and fettered in Gives,' &c.:† and when Posthumus says, 'Cancel these cold bonds,' he means free the soul from the body, as in *Macbeth*, iii. 2,

> *Cancel* and tear to pieces that great *bond*,
> Which keeps me pale!

(where Mr. Staunton plausibly reads *paled*): but the epithet 'cold' has reference to the material gyves, which were of iron: cf. *The Two Noble Kinsmen*, iii. 1, where Palamon says, 'Quit me of these cold gyves'—*i. e.*, knock off my fetters.

Such passages as these two serve as admirable illustrations of the novel position taken by a writer in the *Times* of Sept. 29, 1863, in a review of *The Cambridge Edition of Shakespeare:* 'There never was an author who required less note or comment than Shakespeare.' It is quite true that the mass of readers are content to take the text as they find it, and take in as much of it as they can without trouble; and that the mass of critics and editors are impatient of the restraint which a thorough and

* For the keys to these two passages I am indebted to Mr. Hugh Carleton of Auckland, N.Z., and to the late Rev. W. W. Berry, Prebendary of St. Paul's.

† He is possibly thinking of the *Phaedo,* 72 and 73.

painstaking study of the text would impose upon their con-
jectural fertility — it is so much easier to 'regulate' the text,
or to shun the dark places in it, than to elucidate it. MEAN-
WHILE THE STILL LION IS PATIENT AND LONGSUFFERING, AND
'REQUIRES' NEITHER NOTE NOR COMMENT: BUT IS READY TO
AVENGE HIMSELF ON SCIOLISTS AND MEDDLERS.

We now hold our hand: but passages upon passages crowd
upon us for advocacy and defense, which as yet are suffering
the crying wrongs of emendation. But we trust we have done
enough, both by way of warning and of criticism, to show that
ignorance of the spelling, language, and customs of Shakespeare's
day, is an absolute disqualification for the serious work of verbal
criticism, even more so than the insensibility of such men as
Steevens and Johnson.

The text is beset with difficulties to the ordinary reader,
which are occasioned far more by the presence of obsolete
phraseology and of allusions to obsolete customs and forgotten
events than by the accidents of the press; so that to an ignorant
reader who is impatient of obscurity profuse emendation is a
positive necessity. But unhappily ignorance, insensibility, and
literary ambition concur to convert a reader into a criticaster
of Shakespeare's text. The result is, that passages, eminent
for their sense and beauty, for the purity of their construction,
the selectness of their words, the dignity or fitness of their
thoughts, are defaced and marred by the meddling, clumsy
boor whose vanity has induced him to play the critic. Such
is the fate that has befallen, among many other passages of
faultless excellence, that, perhaps the most lovely of all that

ever flowed from the great soul of the poet, in which Pericles
calls on Helicanus to wound him, lest he should be drowned
with the sweetness of 'the great sea of joys' that rushed upon
him:* till at length we are glad to find a fitting vent for our
grief and indignation in the words of Milton,

> See with what haste these dogs of Hell advance
> To waste and havoc yonder world, which THOU
> Hast made so fair!

---

* We had in mind the late Mr. Samuel Bailey's proposal to alter
'sweetness' into *surges,* for publishing which, in our judgment he deserved
to go woolward and to lie in the woollen, till he came to a better frame of
mind. When we saw his work *On the Received Text of Shakespeare* we
thought we had seen the worst possible of Shakespeare-criticism. We
found ourselves in error there, however, as soon as we saw the now late
Mr. Thomas Keightley's *Shakespeare Expositor.* In defense of Shakespeare's
expression, 'To drown me with their sweetness,' if, forsooth, defense were
needed, or let us say for its illustration, we might cite the following from
Stephen Gosson's *Plays Confuted in Five Actions* (n. d.), sig. B 4, 'because
we are . . . drunken with the sweetness of these vanities.' Here Mr.
Bailey's method of criticism would require us to turn 'sweetness' into
sweetwort, as another critic actually did by 'sweet world' in *King John!*

We may add that in our selection of penances for critical offenses we
have an eye to two passages in Shakespeare which are not always understood.
Those penances are to wear a woollen shirt next the skin, and to sleep
(naked) between the blankets. Sheets served our ancestors for the modern
refinement of a night-dress.

CHAPTER V.

APPY indeed shall we be if our remarks induce the verbal critic to *spare* the works of Shakespeare as he *loves* them. But, at the same time, we concede the fact of textual corruption in many passages, and the probability of corruption in many others. The truth is, that besides the two classes of textual difficulties, called *historical* and *grammatical*, there is a third more formidable than either, viz., the class of *literal* difficulties, which may very well be the result of misprinting. Conjectural criticism being thus allowed, it becomes expedient to assign the limits within which it should be exercised. Something towards this end would be accomplished if a code of rules could be imposed upon all, as a common basis of operations. Evidently, such a preliminary would obviate a vast and useless expenditure of inventive sagacity, and would spare the antiquarians a world of superfluous speculation. There are, indeed, certain considerations which might assist the critics in the determination of that basis ; and, with the object of setting forth these with some approach to systematic treatment, we venture to propound three provisional *canons of emendation*, which severally deal with the three salient features of conjectural criticism: viz., the supposed *crux* itself, the proposed *method* of emending it, and the particular *matter* which is designed to supplant it. In doing this, we disclaim at the outset any overweening confidence in the efficacy of such legislation; for, as it seems to us, however carefully the canons may be drawn up (and on the following three no pains have been spared) there may at any time arise singular cases which, despite the rigour of the canons, are able to establish their right to exceptional treatment.* Still, the code, on the whole, may have its value in checking the licence of conjectural emendation.

In the first place, as a restriction, not disqualification, of the function of conjecture, we would insist upon the supreme duty of deliberation, in lieu of that precipitancy which so often condemns a word as a corruption which is only a difficulty, and has no other fault than that of being *strange, obscure,* or *awkward,* in the place where it stands.

(1)   Evidently a word so unusual as to be unintelligible

---

* Perhaps the following are instances of such.

'Out of *ordeal'd* iron' (Z. Jackson) for 'Out of a great deal of old
     iron.'—1 *Henry IV.*, i. 2.   (Or *ordeal*-iron?)
and
     'I stay but for my *guidon* : to the field !' (G. Thackeray and others)
          for 'I stay but for my guard : On ! to the field!'—*Henry V.*, iv. 2.

and, despite the great difference of *trace,* Mr. ~~G. W.~~ Clark's conjecture of *prospice funem* for 'the prophecy,' in *The Comedy of Errors,* iv. 4, may be a third instance.

may be a perfectly legitimate word: or if not, may be the word intended by the dramatist: indeed it may be an *idiasm* (see p. 40)—a restoration or a coinage of Shakespeare's: in which case it might well be wholly unknown to his critics. With that precipitancy, or disregard of facts, which seems to us so unwise and injurious, a great number of words have been emended for no other reason than their strangeness.

(2) An obscurity in the text may be wholly or partially due to a defect in the critic; as want of knowledge, thought, or perception; and this obscurity may be so profound as to drive him to take refuge in emendation. This has happened in a vast multitude of cases: indeed the highways of criticism are studded with such scarecrows: unhappy felicities of emendation, hung in chains (as it were) for warning to intending marauders. We have furnished several instances of such in Chapter iv. The critical works of the late Mr. Samuel Bailey, the late Mr. Thomas Keightley, and many other recent critics, and the papers in the *Athenæum** of the late Mr. Howard Staunton, will be found to furnish a multitude of examples in point. Similarly, an apparent awkwardness of expression, as unfitness or uncouthness, may also be wholly or partially due to the critic's want of imagination or to his insensibility: and

* These papers, entitled *Unsuspected Corruptions of Shakspeare's Text*, appear in the numbers for Oct. 19 & 26; Nov. 2, 16, & 23; Dec. 14 & 28, 1872: Jan. 25, March 29, April 12, June 14, Nov. 8, Dec. 6, 1873: Jan. 31, March 14, April 4, June 27, 1874. He died on June 22; leaving behind him nothing further than the paper which appeared on June 27, in the same number of the *Athenæum* as that which announced his death. He was our friend of twenty years' standing. We may record that *The Still Lion* provoked his animosity, but did not interrupt our friendship.

the latter may relate to phonetic or to linguistic beauty, or to both. We may summarise these points in the following negative formula.

I. The mere fact of the construction, or a word or words occurring in it, appearing strange, obscure, or awkward, shall not alone constitute a reason for treating the passage as if it were corrupt.

This canon throws upon the critic the paramount duty—so much more difficult than the task of emendation—of *elucidating* and *expounding* every troublesome passage which cannot be proved, beyond question, to be absolute nonsense. The next formula is affirmative, and will justify itself, viz.:

II. The correction of the text shall be attempted upon certain simple hypotheses, framed to account for the supposed misprint, before the adoption of a more sweeping or more violent proceeding; regard being had to the leading or central notion involved in the suspected passage, taken together with its context, and to the phonetic current of the words.

As to the order in which such hypotheses should be tried, there will necessarily be considerable disagreement. We are only stating the result of our own experience of printers' errata, when we assert, that slight literal errors and small dislocations constitute the largest classes; that cases in which letters (or even syllables) are either retrenched or wrongly repeated, are less common than the former; but *far* more frequent than those in which a word is either omitted or wrongly inserted. Such hypotheses, we think, should be exhausted before the critic has recourse to the supposition of a deleted line having been retained in mistake: or of a lost line: and that before entertaining either of those suppositions, it is his duty to consider the possibilities of mishearing or misreading the copy.

A remarkable instance of a suspected line, which one critic would cancel as a line deleted by the author, yet retained by the printer, but another singles out for special eulogy, is in *Anthony and Cleopatra*, v. 2.

> *If idle talk will once be necessary,*
> I'll not sleep neither.

Mr. F. J. Furnivall, on the one hand, is disposed to summarily omit it: Mr. C. J. Monro, in ignorance of such a proposal, regards it as exceptionally felicitous: for he writes to me in these terms of it: 'As to "idle talk"— an amateur is liable to fall in love with particular passages, but I do think *that* a singularly expressive line in its place :' and he paraphrases the entire passage thus: 'If this gift of the gab, which Plutarch will say (for I live before his time) was my particular charm, consents for once to make its "idle talk" humbly useful, it shall be employed in keeping me awake.' Between these two extremes we have various hypotheses for meeting what has been thought a great defect; the more serious of which are Hanmer's and Ritson's proposals to supply a missing line; the former proposing to insert,

> I'll not so much as syllable a word,

the latter, more plausibly, if not more probably, the following line:

> I will not speak; if sleep be necessary,

so as to account for the compositor having skipt a line; while Capell simply treats 'sleep' in the text as a misprint for *speak*. This wholesale method of treatment has been adopted in many other parts of the text in order to recover the whole or a part of a line supposed to be lost through the compositor's eyes wandering to a subsequent line. Here are two examples from the same play (iv. 10):

> order for sea is given;
> They have put forth the haven [   ]
> Where their appointment we may best discover,
> And look on their endeavour.

And again (v. 1),

> The breaking of so great a thing should make
> A greater crack: the round world should have shook,
> [   ] lĭons into civil streets,
> And citizens to their dens.

The hiatus, in each case, has been variously filled up by Rowe, Steevens, and Malone. The old text abounds with passages shewing similar defects.* That whole lines are lost through the compositor's eyes wandering from a word in one line to the same word in a subsequent line, is proved by the known defects of the folio text of 1623 supplied by the earlier quartos, and of the quarto texts supplemented by the folio. In *Troilus and Cressida*, iii. 3, the folios read,

---

* A notable one in *Hamlet*, v. 1, is discussed in the Cambridge Edition of *Shakespeare*, 1866, vol. viii., p. 192, note xxiii.

> The beauty that is borne here in the face
> The bearer knows not, but commends itself
> Not going from itself;

the quartos supplying two lines omitted after the second;

> To other's eyes: nor doth the eye itself,
> That most pure spirit of sense, behold itself,

and in *Hamlet*, ii. 2, the quartos read

> I will leave him and my daughter

omitting the words after ' him,'

> and suddenly contrive the means of meeting between him

which we obtain from the folio. It is fortunate that, in so many plays, we are thus able to supply the defects of the folio by the quartos, and the defects of the quartos by the folio.

Let us suppose now that both these canons are complied with, and the recourse to emendation is justified, there remain over certain considerations which ought to regulate the matter to be substituted for that superseded. There are certain classes of emendations which are not only objectionable, but, however felicitous they may be, can never obtain an unquestioned right to the place in the text: their very hopelessness puts them out of court. This happens—

1. Where there is no close resemblance between the *ductus literarum* of the word or words to be supplanted, and that of the word or words to be supplied, regard being had either to their written or to their printed form. For example: we cannot expect that, in *As You Like It, tributary streams* will ever be

accepted in lieu of 'wearie very means'; that in *All's Well that Ends Well, her own suit joining with her mother's grace,* will ever supplant ' Her insuite comming with her modern grace'; nor yet does it appear likely that, in *The Comedy of Errors, prospice funem* will ever permanently take the place of ' the prophecy.'

2. Where the proposed word is unknown or very unusual in the relative literature: for instance, in 1 *Henry IV., tame chetah* for 'tame cheater'; in *The Tempest, young chamals (i. e.,* Angora goats) for 'young scamels': to which might be added several of the proposed emendations of *strachy* in *Twelfth Night.* At the same time it should be remembered that some words can more readily substantiate their title than others: *e. g., rother* for 'brother' in *Timon of Athens* is a good word enough, and that it was not wholly unknown to Shakespeare is proved by Rother Street in the very town where he was born and died, the name by which the street was known in his life-time. Yet no example of the use of *rother,* an ox, without the addition of *beast,* has ever been discovered in the literature of his day.*

3. Where the proposed word owes its fitness to its possessing a sense or usage which it probably had not so early as the

---

* In 1607 a master in Chancery reports that certain persons are alleged to 'have time out of mind, etc., had herbage and feeding for certain numbers of their *horse beasts* and *roother beasts,*' in respect of ' the Manor of Compton Basset in Com. Wiltes.' (Sir John Tyndall's Report in Lawrence *v.* Merwine, Easter Term, 1607 ; Record Office.) *Roother beasts* occurs some five times more ; *roothers* never ; but *horse beasts* does not occur again ; it is always *horses.* I am indebted to Cecil Monro, Esq., for this extract.

reign of James I: or where the word itself is probably of later introduction. Very great difficulty besets many of these questions of date. As a positive fact *all* the test-words proposed as a royal road to the conviction of the infamous Perkins-imposture have been traced to a date too early for that purpose. (See *A Complete View of the Shakespeare Controversy*, 1861, Chap. vii.) *Wheedle, complaint* (in the medical sense), and even *cheer* (in the applauditory sense, singular number) were probably all in use in the reign of Elizabeth.*

These considerations may be summed up in the following canon.

III. The candidate for admission into the text shall be a legitimate word, known to be in use at the relative time, and otherwise meeting the requirements of the passage, whether as to the leading or central notion, the grammatical construction, or the phonetic syzygy.

Criticism, like Commentary, has often fallen to the lot of men whose abilities and training had not fitted them for that kind of intellectual work. In the fifth of De Quincey's *Letters to a young man whose education has been neglected*, Dr. Nitsch, the Commentator on Kant, affords a mark for the Opium-Eater's fine irony. He fancies the learned doctor protesting against the reasonableness of expecting a man, who has all this commenting to do, to have thoroughly mastered his author.

---

* In Chapter vii. of our *Complete View* we did battle for the test-word proposed by Mr. A. E. Brae. We had better have let it alone. Our opponents did not destroy its credit; but since 1861 we ourselves might have done so. We are now convinced that the Perkins-Folio corrections are too crafty an imposture to admit of such a refutation.

The equitable division of labour demands that one man shall master the system, and another write commentaries! Criticism offers almost as prominent a mark for ridicule. If a few really intelligent and learned men have done much good work in this department, assuredly the greater bulk of criticism has proceeded from those who had few or none of the necessary requirements. The least one might expect of them would be a study of the context, and the reservation of their speculations until some one conjecture can be shown to *stain* its rivals. Nobody cares to be told that possibly a suspicious word in the text is a misprint for this, that, or the other; as is the custom with several critics of this day, to whom the great Becket seems to have bequeathed the rags which served him for a mantle.

The simple truth is, that successful emendation is the fruit of severe study and research on the one hand, and of rare sensibility and sense on the other. The number of really satisfactory conjectures are comparatively few; and few are those critics who have shown any remarkable sagacity in this kind of speculation. The ensuing may be cited with unqualified satisfaction:

1. Our Poesie is a Gowne, which uses
    From whence 'tis nourisht.—*Timon of Athens*, i. 1.
    Our Poesie is a Gumme (Pope) which oozes (Johnson), &c.

2. It is the Pastour Lards, the Brother's sides,
    The want that makes him leaue.—*Ibid.* iv. 3.
    It is the Pasture (Rowe) lards the rother's (Singer) sides,
    The want that makes him leane (Rowe).

3. for thou seest it will not coole my nature.—*Twelfth Night*, i. 3.
   for thou seest it will not curle by (Theobald) nature.

4. Her infuite comming with her moderne grace,
   Subdu'd me to her rate.—*All's Well that Ends Well*, v. 2.
   Her infinite cunning (Walker) &c.

5. Till that the wearie verie meanes do ebbe.—*As You Like It*, ii. 7.
   Till that the wearer's (Singer), &c.

6. To you, our Swords have leaden points, *Mark Antony* :
   Our Armes in strength of malice, and our Hearts
   Of Brothers temper, do receive you in.—*Julius Cæsar*, iii. 1.
   Our Armes in strength of amitie (Singer) &c.*

* Even the proposer of this palmarian emendation was not aware of the corroboration it might receive from Shakespeare's language in other places. We have in *Antony and Cleopatra* the very phrase in one place, and almost the very phrase in another. In ii. 6 we read 'that which is *the strength of their amity* shall prove the immediate author of their variance': and in iii. 2, Antony says,

> I'll *wrestle* with you *in my strength of love.*

Again in 2 *Henry IV.*, 2, we have this parallel,

> Let's drink together friendly, and *embrace,*
> That all their eyes may bear these tokens home
> Of our restored love and *amity* :

We may also strengthen Singer's emendation by the following from *Antony and Cleopatra* : ii. 2, and *Coriolanus* : iv. 5,

> To hold you in perpetual amity,
> To make you brothers, and to knit your hearts
> With an unslipping knot, &c.

> Here I clip
> The anvil of my sword; and do contest,
> As hotly and as nobly with thy love,
> As ever in ambitious strength I did
> Contend against thy valour.

7. Thy paleness moves me more than eloquence.

Merchant of Venice, iii. 2.

Thy plainnesse (Warburton) moves me, &c.

8. For I do see the cruell pangs of death
Right in thine eye.—*King John*, iv. 4.

Riot (Brae) in thine eye.

9. 'Tis enough
That (Britaine) I have kill'd thy Mistris: Peace,
Ile give no wound to thee.—*Cymbeline*, v. 1.

. . . . I have kill'd thy Mistris-piece (Staunton).*

* This masterpiece in emendation was communicated to us by Mr. Staunton in the course of conversation, shortly after the completion of his Edition of Shakespeare. He thought himself supported in this correction by an expression in *The Winter's Tale*, i. 2 :

I love thee not a jar o' the clock behind
What lady she her lord.

where he reads *lady-she*. We marvel at Mr. Abbott's adoption of this reading (*Shakespearean Grammar*, 1870, pp. 149, note, and 174: *i. e.*, §§ 225 and 255); while his gloss, explaining a *lady-she* to be 'a well-born woman' (as if that were something more than a *lady*) seems to us to verge on the ridiculous. On the contrary, a *mistress-piece* is chief lady, a lady who is mistress of all ladyhood. In our opinion, 'behind what lady she her lord,' means 'less than any lady whatsoever [loves] her lord.' cf. *e. g.*,

The King he takes the babe
To his protection.—*Cymbeline*, i. 1.

the chain
Which God he knows I saw not.—*Comedy of Errors*, v. 1.

Thy rod and thy staff they comfort me.—*Ps.* xxiii, 4.

God he knowes how many men's lives it will cost, &c.

Powell's *Art of Thriving*. 1635.

But though the passage in *The Winter's Tale* affords no corroboration of Mr. Staunton's emendation in *Cymbeline*, the following from Ford's *Lady's Trial*, i. 2, does support it :

him we have beleaguer'd to accost
This *she-piece*.

10. for his Nose was as sharpe as a Pen, and a Table of greene fields.
Henry V., ii. 3.
. . . . . . and a Babled (Theobald) of greene fields.

11. If every of your wishes had a wombe
And foretell every wish, a Million.—*Antony and Cleopatra*, i. 2.
And fertile every wish (Warburton).

12.   Oh then we bring forth weeds,
When our quicke windes lye still.—*Ibid.*
When our quicke *mindes*, &c. (Warburton)

13. Then would thou hadst a paire of chaps, no more,
And throw betweene them all the food thou hast,
They'll grinde the other. Where's *Antony?*
Antony and Cleopatra, iii. 5.
Then world, thou hast, &c.
They'll grinde the one the other (Johnson).

14.   For his Bounty,
There was no winter in't. An *Anthony* it was,
That grew the more by reaping.—*Antony and Cleopatra*, v. 2.
an autumn 'twas (Theobald).

15. I have retyr'd me to a wastefull cocke.—*Timon of Athens*, ii. 2.
I have retyr'd me to a wakefull couche (Swynfen Jervis).

As to the last, a few remarks may be added in justification of so valuable a correction. We do not touch the fitness or the beauty of the emendation, which speak for themselves, but we insist upon the probability of the misprint. We must use the favourite resource of Zachary Jackson here. In the 'upper case' of the compositor, the ſt and k are in contiguous 'boxes,' so that an ſt would sometimes be dropped into the k box by mistake: thus | ſt | k |; whence it might very well happen that *wakefull* was set up *waſtefull*. Not improbably, *wakefull* in the 'copy' suggested *cock* to the mind of the workman instead of *couch*, by the power of association; the barn-cock being often called the wakeful bird, or the wakeful cock. As an illustration of this particular misprint, we may cite these two instances: in one Birmingham newspaper we observed the remarkable expression (of a remarkable phenomenon) 'sermon without bosh,' which we were told was an error for 'sermon without *book;*' and in another, 'genial break' for 'genial *breath;*' and the blunder of 'break' for *breath* also occurred in one of the proofs of our tractate entitled, *Was Thomas Lodge an Actor ?* p. 10.

Of course, in order to appreciate the actual duty done by each of these fifteen emendations, it is necessary to make the passage to which it applies a special study. All that the mere presentation of them to the eye can do, is to show the reader that the *ductus literarum* of the conjecture is sufficiently near to that of the text, which is also the case with the majority of unsuccessful conjectures.

As in the substitution of 'wastefull' for *wakefull*, in many misprints the process is patent: we see, for instance (Ex. 6), that the misprint 'malice' arose from the compositor setting up *amitie* awry, and transposing the *m* and *a*. Again (Ex. 8 and 9), we see that 'Right' and 'Peace' probably arose from mishearing the genuine word. In some cases, however, we see the fatality under which certain classes of words were wrongly set up, without being able to see why that fatality existed. Of all classes pronouns (simply as such) were the most commonly

misprinted.* The first folio of Shakespeare and the first quarto
of the *Sonnets* teem with such errors.   Some particular passages
seem to have suffered from a similar fatality.   Again and again
has corruption disastered them, misprint being graffed on
misprint.   Here are two examples :

---

   * A most important instance is given on p. ⟨⟩ *ante.*   With the utmost
diffidence we suggest another, in *Macbeth*, ii. 2 :

> no : this my Hand will rather
> The multitudinous Seas incarnadine,
> Making the Greene one, Red.   (*sic* in fo. 1623.)

Read, *nostro periculo,*

'Making *their* Greene, one Red': *i. e.*, making the green *of the multitu-*
dinous seas an universal red—'total gules.'   This very slight change oblit-
erates the defect which Mr. Staunton found in the third line, viz., that
'the Greene' (apart from 'one') cannot be a substantive expression : which
was his excuse for a most violent and less satisfactory alteration.

   The converse misprint of 'their' for *the*, occurs in *Antony and Cleopatra*,
ii. 2.

> Her Gentlewomen, like the Nereides,
> So many Mer-maides tended her i' th' eyes,
> And made their bends adornings.   At the Helme
> A seeming Mer-maide steers :

Where we read, after Zachary Jackson, '*the* bends' adornings.'   Both
'eyes' and 'bends' were parts of Cleopatra's barge.   The *eyes* of a ship
are the hawseholes : the *bends* are the wales, or thickest planks in the
ship's sides.   North has it : 'others tending the tackle and ropes of the
barge ;' which settles the question as to the meaning of *eyes :* and that once
fixed, the other part of the interpretation is inevitable.   What could the
hardy soldier, Enobarbus, care for the curves of the mermaid's bodies ?   To
us it is obvious that if the girls tended Cleopatra at the eyes, they would,
there, be the natural ornaments of the bends.   Even Mr. Dyce, in his latest
edition, failed to see the obvious meaning of this passage.

1. In the *Tempest*, i. 2, it is beyond the shadow of a doubt
that Shakespeare wrote,

> Urchins
> Shall forth at vast of night, that they may worke
> All exercise on thee.

Three morsels of knowledge, indeed, are requisite for the full
comprehension of the sense : *to forth* was a common phrase
for *to go forth; vast of night* meant *dead of night;* and *exercise*
meant *chastisement* or *penance*, as in *Othello*, iii. 4.   Ignorance
of one or some of these things has hitherto hindered the
reception of Mr. Thomas White's restoration.   It has been
argued by a very competent critic and editor, that *exercise*
must be a verb, because *to work exercise* would, otherwise,
be a pleonasm which it would be impertinent to impute to
Shakespeare.   Nothing can be more fallacious than that style
of argument.   Pleonasms are the very stuff of the Elizabethan
and Jacobian writers.   In our authorized version of the Holy
Scriptures, for instance, St. Paul is made to say (2 Cor. viii. 11),
' Now therefore, perform ye the doing of it.'   But nevertheless,
to work an exercise is not a pleonasm : it means *to perform
a penal act:* ' that they may worke all exercise on thee,'
therefore means, ' that they may perform on thee all the
penalties I have allotted them.'   Unhappily in setting up the
text of the *Tempest* in 1622, the ' th' of ' forth' got slightly
dislocated, so as to be too near the following word ' at.'
Accordingly, the lines stand there

> Urchins
> Shall for that vast of night, that they may worke
> All exercise on thee.

Then came the editors who, seeing in the line in question an intimation of the awfully indefinite duration of the night during which ~~the~~ urchins are permitted to exercise the infernal arts on Caliban—as if, forsooth, their privilege were limited to a single night, and to one which was longer than any other—advanced the limitary comma from 'night' to 'worke.' Then came Thomas Warton, who, requiring the line for the illustration of one in Milton, gave it in a note thus:

> Urchins
> Shall for that want of night that they may work;

thereby graffing one misprint on another. *

2. In *Timon of Athens*, i. 1, Shakespeare undoubtedly wrote,

> Our poesie is as a gumme which oozes
> From whence 'tis nourisht.

But in the edition of 1623 the passage was, as we have seen, thus misprinted,

> Our Poesie is as a Gowne which uses
> From whence 'tis nourisht.

and Tieck, who set himself up as a critic on Shakespeare and other English Dramatists, defended the nonsense, under the impression, perhaps, that Shakespeare meant to compare poetry to a worn-out robe! Unhappy passage! In a letter on 'The influences of Newspapers on Education,' written by Mr. Blanchard Jerrold, in the *Daily News*, he had intended to

---

* In the German edition of *The Still Lion* the line appears with a new misprint,

Shall forth at vast of night, that they make worke. See *ante*, p. 39.

quote the amended version ; but to his horror it appeared in a totally new form,

> Our poesy is as a queen that dozeth ;

and it now remains for some conceited foreigner of the future to contend that the bard meant to signalize the drowsiness of our poetry, by comparing it to a queen, who, despite the calls of her high station, falls asleep on her throne !

Let us now consider three selected passages, given in both the quarto and folio editions of *Hamlet.* These will serve as samples (additional to those on p. 111) of the state of the old text, and of the value of having more than one version of a passage which has suffered from the blunder of copyist or printer. In the first, the folio corrects the error of the quarto : in the second, the quarto corrects the error of the folio : in the third, the folio deserts us ; no quarto-reading can, in this case, be allowed as the correction of another ; and conjecture has not arrived at any satisfactory result.

1. In *Hamlet,* iv. 7, as given in the quartos of 1604 and 1605, we have,

> so that my arrowes
> Too slightly tymberd for so loued Arm'd,
> Would have reuerted to my bowe againe,
> But not where I haue [had] aym'd them.

The only variation in the words 'loued Arm'd' given by the early quartos is, that two read 'loued armes,' and one reads 'loved armes.'

Such a crux as that would have been 'larks' or 'nuts' to the critical taste. Happily the folio 1623 gives us the true

lection, viz., *loud a Winde.* So Ascham, in his *Toxophilus,*
book ii. (Arber's Reprint, p. 150-1), says, ' The greatest enemy
of Shootyng is the winde and wether, &c. Weak bowes, and
lyght shaftes can not stande in a rough wynde.'

2. If, on the other hand, we had but the first folio, we
should be called upon to *explain* or *amend* the following passage
in *Hamlet:*

> To his good Friends, thus wide Ile ope my Armes:
> And like the kinde Life-rend'ring Politician,
> Repast them with my blood.

Such a crux as ' Life-rend'ring Politician' would have been
as appetising and entertaining as the last; and the game would
naturally have been quickened by the fact, that when *Hamlet*
was first indited *Politician,* occurring once, however, in this
play ('the Pate of a Politician,' iv. 1), was an *insolens verbum,*
which we now believe to have been first used by George
Puttenham in 1589, if he were the author (which he probably
was) of *The Arte of English Poesie.* The misprint is an unusual
expansion of the original word. It is most unlikely that *Pelican*
(the word of the quarto editions) was (as some have asserted) a
difficulty with the old compositor: on the contrary, we may be
pretty sure that he set up *Polician,* and that a pedantic ' reader'
of the house improved upon this, converting it into *Politician.*

3. Now for a case in which the old copies concur to
leave us at the mercy of conjecture. In the same quarto
editions of *Hamlet* we read,

> For use almost can change the stamp of nature,
> And either the devill, or throwe him out
> With wonderous potency.

Unhappily this passage, defective by *one* word (probably a verb following on 'either' and governing 'the devill'), is not in the first quarto, nor yet in any of the early folio editions. The defect is so miserably supplied by the dateless quarto (1607) that the modern editor is driven to the conclusion that the word there given is a mere conjecture, and that the defect must be anew conjecturally supplied. This quarto reads :—

> For use almost can change the stamp of nature,
> And maister the devill, or throwe him out
> With wonderous potency.

Here 'maister' is not only bad on the score of rhythm, but still leaves the line short. Not improbably it was intended to supply the word for which 'either' was conceived to be a misprint. Pope and Capell followed this lead, and read 'And master *even* the devil —' But all other editors have wisely retained 'either': viz., 'And either *curb* the devil'— Malone; 'And either *quell* the devil'— Singer: while the late Mr. Bolton Corney proposed to read, 'And either *aid* the devil'— and Mr. Cartwright, 'And either *lay* the devil.' A correspondent of *Notes and Queries* (3rd S. x. 426) signing himself F., proposed, 'And either *house* the devil'; conceiving (like Mr. Corney) that the missing word should be antithetical to *throw out,* and not perceiving that no very 'wondrous potency' would be required to house a demon, who was already by nature in possession! The Cambridge editors favour *couch* and *lodge;* both words being found in Harsnet's *Declaration,* c. 12, the former in the sense of *subdue,* the latter in the sense of *confine*. (Clarendon Press Edition of *Hamlet*, p. 189-190.) Two other conjectures privately communicated to us deserve mention. Our valued friend, Professor Sylvester, proposed to read, 'And either *mask* the devil'—conceiving that 'maister' might be a misprint for the true word. In this course he is somewhat countenanced by a passage occurring in a prior speech of Polonius (iii. 1):

> We are oft to blame in this,—
> 'Tis too much proved, that with devotion's visage,
> And pious action, we do sugar o'er
> The devil himself.

Another valued friend, Mr. C. J. Monro, half-seriously suggested, 'And *entertain* the devil'—conceiving that 'either' might be a press error for *entertain*. All other conjectures which I have seen are so utterly imbecile, that I will spare their proposers the ordeal of criticism. It is not easy to discover why the seven verbs, *curb, quell, lay, aid, house, couch,* and *lodge* should find more favour than a score of others, apparently as well suited to the sense and measure of the line as any of those. How soon are the resources of the conjectural critics exhausted! how meagre is the evidence adduced in favour of any single conjecture! Yet the requirements of the passage are by no means severe, nor are the means for complying with them either narrow or *recherché*. It is rather an *embarras des richesses* that hinders ours decision. To call over a few of the candidates for admission into the text : *curb* suggests *rein, rule, thrall, bind, chain,* &c.; *quell, lay,* and *couch* suggest *charm, worst, quench, foil, balk, cross, thwart, daunt, shame, cow, tame*, &c. ; while *aid* suggests *fire, rouse, stir, serve, feed*, &c. Besides which there are many dissyllables that would answer the purposes of sense and measure, as *abate, abase*, &c. And why not read, 'And over-maister the devil'— seeing that the word *o'ermaster* occurs in a former scene of this play? We are not now attempting the settlement of this question, but merely pointing out what a wealth of suggestion has been ignored by the self-complacent critics who have so feebly attempted it. But as a preliminary to its settlement, we venture to call attention to the evident requirements of the passage. 'The stamp of nature' is not new to us in this connection, nor in this play; we have had it twice in the second ghost-scene, viz., the 'vicious mole of nature,' and 'the stamp of one defect.' Now Hamlet would say, 'Use almost can change, or convert, this stamp of nature': so that an antithesis is not only *not* required, but is impertinent. Use, he would say, can either *subdue* 'habit's devil,' by following out his own prescription of *gradual weaning from evil*, or (if the worst come to the worst and revolution be necessary) *cast him out:* and either of these can such use, or change of habit, effect 'with wondrous potency.' The key-note of the whole passage is 'Reformation, by gradually subduing evil habits'; and so far from Hamlet's advice, 'assume a virtue if you have it not,' being (as Charles Knight understood it) a recommendation of hypocrisy, 'the homage paid by vice to virtue,' it is given solely with the view of facilitating inward amendment, and is therefore honest and sincere. Very similar advice was given by Lewis Vives in a book which, not improbably, may have been Shakespeare's closet-companion, viz., *The Introduction to Wysedom:* Englished by [Sir] Richarde Morysine: 1540, Sig. B ii.

> ' Let every man desyre uprighte thinges, and flee the crooked: chose the good, and refuse the evyll, *this use and custome shall tourne well doinge almost into nature,* and so worke, that none, but suche as are compelled, and suche as are in stryfe, found the weaker, shall be brought to do evyll.'

Roger Ascham, too, in his *Toxophilus,* 1545, book ii. (Arber's Reprint, p. 141), has the same proposition in somewhat different words . . . .

> ' And in stede of the fervent desyre, which provoketh a chylde to be better than hys felowe, lette a man be as muche stirred up with shamefastnes to be worse than all other. * * * * * And hereby you may se that that is true whiche Cicero sayeth, *that a man by use, may be broughte to a newe nature.'*

This, in fact, is exactly what is meant in Sir Joshua Reynolds' *Fifteenth Discourse,* where we are recommended ' to feign a relish till we find a relish come, and feel that what began in fiction terminates in reality': and Sir Walter Scott, in the *Bride of Lammermoor,* chapter vi., observes, ' that when a man commences by acting a character, he frequently ends by adopting it in good earnest.'

The missing word, then, must at least import *the subduing of the devil of habit.* In the first quarto we have the expression,

> ' And win [*i. e.,* wean] yourself by little as you may,'

from the sin to which you [the queen] have habituated yourself. Now, that *weaning by little and little,* or gradually weaning the will and affections from the customary sin, 'recurring and suggesting still,' is just what the missing word, were it recovered, would assuredly be found to express or to imply. *Lay* and *shame* are equally acceptable in sense, and both afford a perfect rhythm. Perhaps *shame* is the finer reading of the two. At the same time, it must be owned, that Hamlet's prescription is calculated to do but little for the sinner: at best, we fear, to 'skin and film the ulcerous place.' Kant well says:

> 'People usually set about this matter [*i. e.,* the reformation of character] otherwise, fighting against particular vices, and leaving the common root whence they sprout untouched. And yet mankind   *   *   *   is just so much the more readily awakened to a profounder reverence for duty, the more he is taught to exclude therefrom all foreign motives that self-love might foist into the maxims of conduct.'

We can hardly say that conjecture has yet determined the best reading here; though it cannot be said that sufficient indications are wanting for its guidance. Unfortunately it is in the very nature of the case, that some doubt should continue to vex this passage, after conjecture has done its work.

Let us take a more striking case than this: a passage in which there is no *hiatus:* merely a misprint; which has nevertheless all the features of incurable corruption. We refer to that famous Rope-scarre which occurs at the opening of the fifth act of *Much Ado about Nothing.* Leonato, refusing the proffered consolations of his brother, says,

> Bring me a father that so lov'd his childe,
> Whose joy of her is overwhelm'd like mine,
> And bid him speake of patience.

Ritson reads the last line,

> And bid him speake *to me* of patience,

and the late Mr. Barron Field independently suggested the same unnecessary, if not impertinent, interpolation. Leonato continues, after four lines which we omit here,

> If such a one will smile and stroke his beard,
> And sorrow, wagge, crie hem, when he should grone,
> Patch grief with proverbs, make misfortune drunke,
> With candle-wasters: bring him yet to me,
> And I of him will gather patience:
> But there is no such man, &c. (Fo. 1623.)

The line, 'And I *of him* will gather patience,' doubtless suggested the conjecture of Ritson and Barron Field. The argument is this: ' Find me a man who has suffered my calamity; and if he will speak of patience, I, on my part, will gather patience of him.' In the passage lately quoted there are two difficulties. The first was plausibly bridged over by Steevens by simply transposing 'And' and 'crie,' 'wagge' meaning, according to this interpretation, as it does in so many other places, *budge.* The objection to this is, that it hardly comports with the bland and philosophic character of the person whom Leonatus invests with his own wrongs and sorrows. The second difficulty concerns the obsolete word ' candle-wasters.'

s

Here, then, is a passage which demands both emendation and exposition: but in order to deal with it successfully, we must first cope with the second difficulty. Of all the commentators, Zachary Jackson alone proposed an emendation for ' candle-wasters': he conjectured *caudle-waters !* What it means is hard to say; for no such word is known to have ever existed, though *caudle*, a sort of posset, is familiar enough. We remember that Eden Warwick (*i. e.,* the late Mr. George Jabet, the accomplished editor of *The Poet's Pleasaunce*, 1847) proposed in *Notes and Queries* to substitute for Hamlet's *pajock* or *paiocke* the strange word *patokie,* a word he had coined expressly for the occasion, as a possible derivative of *patacco* or *patoikoi.* We need not pause to consider the merit or demerit of such singular suggestions, both being non-suited for something much worse than *insolentia.* But, regarding ' candle-wasters ' as a genuine word, what was its meaning? Mr. Staunton (Ed. vol. i., p. 730) says that it means 'Bacchanals, revellers.' Mr. Dyce follows suit. I venture to think that these editors have gone beyond the voucher of their authorities. We do not believe that a single example can be adduced of *candle-waster* in that sense.

It is to us passing strange that the word ' drunk ' in this passage should have been uniformly interpreted in its literal sense, and ' candle-wasters ' understood to mean drunkards, who spend the night in revelling. There are few things more painfully absurd than the attempt to literalize a metaphor. Surely Shakespeare never meant Leonato to deny the possibility of drowning trouble in drink; for that were the easiest as it is the ordinary resource of a vulgar man in trouble. Nanty

Ewart, in *Redgauntlet,* is such a man. Drunkenness was his resource from the misery of haunting memories. ' Here is no lack of my best friend,' said Ewart, on taking out his flask, after awakening an old sorrow, the remembrance of which was too painful to be borne with patience. Whatever, then, was meant by ' making misfortune drunk with candle-wasters,' it must have been some achievement which in Leonato's circumstances was very difficult of performance; so difficult that he pronounced it impossible. Now, Whalley succeeded in unearthing two examples of the use of *candle-waster* and *lamp-waster,* and one of *candle-wasting,* which throw considerable light on this passage; but which, from their rebutting the ordinary interpretation, are usually suppressed by the editors. Here they are :

Heart, was there ever so prosperous an invention thus unluckily prevented and spoiled by a whoreson book-worm or *candle-waster?*
Ben Johnson: *Cynthia's Revells*, iii. **2.**

He should more catch your delicate court-ear, than all your head-scratchers, thumb-biters, *lamp-wasters* of them all.
Shakerley Marmion: *The Antiquary,* 1641, 4to.

I which have known you better and more inwardly than a thousand of these *candle-wasting* book-worms.
The Hospitall of Incurable Fooles: Erected in English, as near the first Italian modell and platforme, as the unskilfull hand of an ignorant Architect could devise. 1600, sm. 4to. Sig. H.

From these extracts we gather that a *candle-waster* is a *book-worm;* literally, a consumer of 'the midnight oil,' a nocturnal student; and the term (like ' Grub-street '.of a century later) was always applied contemptuously, and the work of such

a writer was said, after the Latin phrase, *to smell of the lamp.**
Not improbably the term meant also a *lucubration.*   The conclusion is, that *to make misfortune drunk with candle-wasters,* is
to drown one's troubles in study; and what fitter pendant could
be found to the preceding phrase to 'patch grief with proverbs'?

So far, then, all is clear and indisputable.   We may now
recur to the former part of Leonato's speech, in which the real
crux lies:

> If such a one will smile and stroke his beard,
> And sorrow, wagge, crie hem, when he should grone, &c.

To stroke the beard and cry hem! (what the French call *faire
le sérieux*) is the very picture of a sententious pedant who
would talk down or scold down the first gush of natural feeling,
whether of grief or of rage.   Such was Achilles' epitome of
Nestor in *Troilus and Cressida,* i. 3, where that chief is described
as amusing himself with Patroclus' mimicry of the Greeks :

> Now play me Nestor; hem and stroke thy beard !

And if any doubt still remained that Shakespeare, by the expression 'stroke his beard,' meant to describe a philosophic
character, the following, from a comedy of the time, would
remove it: viz.,

---

* *Lucernam olet.*   Again, *Oleum perdere* is to lose one's labour in
writing, to be an oil-waster.   Dryden, in his Preface to *Troilus and Cressida,*
1679, 8vo, falls foul of Shakespeare for *catachresis;* and in the same breath
speaks of certain dramas smelling of the buskin!   As buskins are not
remarkable for their offensive odour, the phrase is a worse *catachresis* than
is to be found in Shakespeare.   By the way, 'drunk with candle-wasting,'
would be a more natural expression.

Yes, thou shalt now see me stroke my beard, and speake sententiously.
Chapman's *May Day*, ii. 1.

It seems to follow, then, that the words, 'And sorrow wagge,' must be an error for some phrase expressive of choking, smothering, or suppressing sorrow. Hence we venture to think, that, supposing there has been no dislocation of the text, Tyrwhitt's conjecture of *gagge* for 'wagge' at least preserves the continuity of the thought, and the integrity of the image, as well as the *ductus literarum*. Such a metaphor, too, is not more extraordinary than Shakespeare's use of *strangle* in several passages: *e. g.*,

Strangle such thoughts in thee.—*The Winter's Tale*, iv. 3.

To attempt to settle the question definitely in favour of this or that conjecture would at present be mere waste of time. The interpretation we have given to the purport of the passage cannot, we are assured, be successfully assailed; and that may help the critic to a solution of the textual difficulty.

Mr. Staunton, who found, as we have said, a bacchanial allusion in the phrase, *to make misfortune drunk with candle-wasters*, persuaded himself that the former part of the speech bore out that view. He contended that to 'cry hem' here means, to sing the burden of a roystering song.* To all which

---

* Possibly 'Hem, boys!' in 2 *Henry IV.*, iii. 2, is part of such a refrain. But *to hem* also meant to feign indifference: *e. g.*,

Ros. I could shake them off my coat; these burs are in my heart.
Cel. Hem them away.
Ros. I would try; if I could cry *hem*, and have *him*.
As You Like It, i. 3.

we say, (1) that no example of either the one or the other phrase, employed in those senses has ever been adduced; (2) that if a dozen examples in point were found, the case would be in no wise mended; for the interpretation in question is logically inconsistent with the context. The counsel Leonato is rejecting, is that he should seek to restrain and assuage his grief, rather than indulge it. To reply, as we contend he is intended to do, 'Show me a man who has my weight of sorrow and wrong, and is yet an example of stoical or cheerful endurance, and I will follow your counsel,' is logical and *ad rem:* but to reply, 'Show me a man who, having as great a sorrow or wrong as I have, drowns the remembrance of it in drunken revelry,' &c., would be wholly irrelevant: and this for four reasons, which are here set forth at length:

i. Because it would imply that Antonio had been recommending drunkenness to his brother, as an infallible specific for grief: for it would make Leonato's words imply that if a man could be produced who had succeeded in that feat, he would accede to his brother's suggestion, and make such a man his model: only 'patience' would be an outstanding difficulty.

ii. Because it would make Leonato say, 'Show me a man who has so little patience and self-control as to rush to the tap-room for the solace of his troubles, and I will make him my model, and gather patience of him,' which would be an impossible task.

iii. Because it would make him assert that there is no such man: that no man could be found who, having Leonato's sorrow or wrong, could succeed in forgetting it in drinking-bouts: whereas drink is, as we have seen, the common resource of common men in trouble.

iv. Because it would confound the intellectual man with him who lacks intellect, industry, and moral feeling. As Mrs. Beecher-Stowe so well puts it in *Dred* (chap. x.), ' Every one [who is ' uncomfortable and gloomy'] naturally inclines towards *some* source of consolation. *He who is intellectual reads and studies;* he who is industrious flies to business; he who is affectionate seeks friends; he who is pious, religion; *but he who is none of these—what has he but his whiskey ?* ' It is thus that the common sense of our time throws light upon the dark or doubtful passages in Shakespeare. But this particular *crux* is, in our opinion, one of the least doubtful *in drift*, though it has been so persistently perverted by commentators of the literalizing school.

We may here cite a few other instances of the supreme value of modern illustration, as an aid to emendation and interpretation (we gave several at pp. 82, 98, 127 and 131). We have already noted the plausibility of *bed* as an emendation of ' bone ' in that famous speech of Alcibiades, which Mr. Dyce printed without an attempt to defend or explain it. Addressing the doting senators (behind their backs), the general exclaims,

> Now the Gods keepe you old enough,
> That you may live
> Onely in bone, that none may looke on you.
>
> *Timon*, iii. 5. (Fo. 1623.)

That the *one* in ' bone ' was caught by the compositor from the *one* in 'onely,' is probable, regard being had to the prox-imity of 'none.' Surely, their fitting place was *bed*, where the ailments of their advanced age might receive all needful minis-trations, and where they would also be safe from bringing disgrace on the government of Athens. In this reading we are supported by a passage in Mr. George Dawson's address to his congregation, on the occasion of celebrating the twenty-fifth anniversary of 'The Church of the Saviour' at Birmingham, delivered there on August 5, 1872. He said, in reference to his own late illness,

> 'To be patient with a man who has always something the matter with him is one of the grandest kinds of patience. People always ailing are tiresome, there is no denying it. I have a great dread of becoming an invalid. I have a great respect for invalids *in bed—out of sight.*'

i. e., 'Only in bed, that none may look on [them].' Can a more light-giving illustration be conceived?

Then, apart from emendation, how 'express and admirable' is the following from a modern novelist, now deceased, as deter-mining the sense of an obscure phrase in *Hamlet*, i. 1. Bernardo asks,

> 'What, is Horatio there?'

To which Horatio replies,

> 'A piece of him.'

The late Charles Knight speaks of this as Horatio's 'familiar pleasantry': but what is its meaning? The simple answer is—Horatio calls his hand, as he touches that of the soldier—a piece of himself, because he could not be distinctly seen in the dark shade of the battlement: *i. e.*, a piece, as implying that the rest was there, though not revealed to ~~Hamlet's~~ sense at once. Now all this is suggested by a passage in the penultimate chapter of *Jane Eyre.* She has come upon the blind Rochester, and placed her hand in his:

> 'Her very fingers,' he cried, 'her small, slight fingers! *If so, there must be more of her.*'

Of course, neither Charlotte Brontë nor Mr. George Dawson had the faintest notion of illustrating Shakespeare, when these things were uttered. If either of them had, some of the force of the illustration would be lost. As it is, we here see the power of common sense, even in this day, to do the great playwright yeoman's service.

Just so does a fine passage in Mr. Caird's sermon, entitled *Religion in Common Life,* p. 24, afford a guiding light for all who care to determine the exact thought which was in Shakespeare's mind when he wrote that passage in the *Tempest,* iii. 1, which is so corruptly given in the folio 1623:

> I forget;
> But these sweet thoughts, doe even refresh my labours,
> Most busie lest, when I doe it.

Mr. Caird says,

> 'The thought of all this may dwell, a latent joy, a hidden motive, deep down in his heart of hearts, may come rushing in, a sweet solace, *at every pause of exertion,* and act like a

T

secret oil to smooth the wheels of labour.' Certainly Shakespeare meant to say that *the sweet thoughts well up in the pauses of exertion.* Had not Dr. Wellesley overlooked this, he would not have applied 'most' to 'refresh,' and 'busy' to Ferdinand (*Stray Notes*, 1865, p. 2), making him say that his sweet thoughts refresh him by their presence during his labours. We would adopt Mr. Bullock's reading, *busiliest* for 'busie lest,' and regulate the passage thus:

> I forget [*i. e.*, I am forgetting my injunction],
> But these sweet thoughts doe even refresh my labours
> Most busiliest when I doe it. [*i. e.*, do forget it.]

Busiliest may have been written *busielest* (we note that *easiliest* is printed *easilest* in *Cymbeline*, iv. 2, fo. 1623): and if so the only error in the folio is a slight dislocation in that word. We observe, too, that this play presents several instances of comparatives so formed from adverbs: *e. g.*,

> You have taken it *wiselier* than I meant you should.—*Tempest*, iii, 2.

> ✳ ✳ ✳ and shall not myself
> ✳ ✳ ✳ be *kindlier* moved than thou art?—*Ibid.*, v. 1.

But here, as in the *crux* from *Much Ado about Nothing*, the question does not admit of a final decision. In such, and the like, we must be content to suspend our judgment, and exercise patience.

Once more, in that sublime passage in the *Tempest*, iv. 1, on the instability of the sensible universe, three or four injurious and impertinent alterations have been unsuccess-

fully attempted : as *wrack* and *track* for 'rack'; *brittle* for
'little'; &c.: and Warburton's gloss on a misprint of the
second folio (viz., *th'air* for *their*, as 'this' appeared in 1632).
Besides which M. François V. Hugo renders the phrase 'all
which it inherit' (where 'it' is the objective to 'inherit') *tout ce
qu'il contient*, thus converting 'inherit' into *inherits*. Meanwhile
it is absolutely certain that the entire passage is absolutely
fleckless and flawless, as it stands in the first folio. Hardly
in all Shakespeare can two or three successive lines be found
more touchingly beautiful than these (we are disposed to accept
Steevens' alteration of 'on' into *of*) :

> We are such stuff
> As dreams are made of, and our little life
> Is rounded with a sleep.

To seize the central or leading notion here is not difficult.
Jean Paul—a man worthy to be Shakespeare's unconscious
interpreter—was certainly not thinking of this fine passage
when he wrote the following in *Flower, Fruit, and Thorn-pieces*,
chapter xv.: which I quote from Mr. E. H. Noel's admirable
version.

> 'And he thought of the clouds, the cold and the night,
> that reigned *around the poles of life*—the birth and death
> of man—as round the poles of the earth.'

What does this mean, but that our life is rounded by the sleep
of birth and death: as if they were its poles? And ours is but
a *little* life: but little is included between those poles, so little,

that we thank God that the later pole is but a sleep. The accomplished author of *Lorna Doone* thus freely (and legitimately) employs Shakespeare's image: only there is one word which one might wish expunged: viz., ' off ' before ' of.'

> ' In the farthest and darkest nook overgrown with grass, and overhung by a weeping tree, a little bank of earth betokened *the rounding off of a hapless life.'—Lorna Doone*, chap. lvii.

In a multitude of cases, however, the correction of the text is certain; and in some, where the remedy is still somewhat doubtful, a particular emendation which has met with all but universal acceptance by the editors has been now and then pronounced too good for the place! It is an exceptional honour for the conjectural critic to be esteemed almost equal to his author. Such was the approbation bestowed by Dr. Johnson on Warburton for his emendation of *God, vice* ' good,' in *Hamlet*, ii. 2: ' being a good kissing carrion'; but surely approbation was never so extravagant as in this opinion; for, as Mr. Corson points out, ' a good kissing carrion' is simply a carrion that is good for kissing! The highest honour, however, attainable by the author of an emendation was actually attained by Theobald, viz., that of being confounded with his author, and that by no ordinary critic. In our opinion he fully deserved that honour, and stands *facile princeps* among the host of conjectural critics. Holding that opinion, we indignantly repel Dr. Johnson's censure on Theobald; whom he calls ' a man of narrow comprehension and small acquisitions, with no

native and intrinsic splendour of genius, with little of the arti-
ficial light of learning, but zealous for minute accuracy, and
not negligent in pursuing it.' But, as if grudging Theobald
this small concession, he adds that Theobald was weak and
ignorant,' 'mean and faithless,' 'petulant and ostentatious.'
De Quincey, echoing Johnson, calls Theobald 'painstaking but
dull' (*Works*, Black, vol. vi. p. 126, note); and yet, on another
occasion, when De Quincey is insisting on 'the gratitude of
our veneration for Shakespeare,' he actually adduces, as a remarkable display of Shakespeare's dramatic art, the famous
words, 'and a babled of green fields,' from Mrs. Quickly's
description of Falstaff's death, in *Henry V.*, ii. 3. Those words,
he thinks, 'must have been read by many a thousand with tears
and smiles at the same instant'; 'I mean,' he adds, 'connecting
them with a previous knowledge of Falstaff and of Mrs. Quickly.'
(*Works*, Black, vol. xiii. p. 119.) Just so: that is precisely
where lies the marvel of this piece of work, which we owe to
Theobald rather than to Shakespeare. We are far from denying
that those words are what Shakespeare wrote: indeed it is
the peculiar merit of that emendation that most probably it
exactly restores the original work of the bard : but Theobald
had to work upon the corrupt text, 'and a Table of greene
fields,' which seems to promise so little poetry or knowledge
of human nature, that one critic is satisfied that they are a
stage direction, incorporated, by mistake, with the text of Mrs.
Quickly's speech ; another supposes the reference to be to a
pen lying on a table-book of green fell ; while Mr. Collier's
pseudo-old Corrector alters the words into ' on a table of

green frieze.'*   Hopeless indeed must the prosaic corruption
appear to most men—to all who have not caught the infection
of Shakespeare's genius, and have not a like knowledge of
human nature.   Theobald however, proved himself to have
had both.   He knew precisely how Falstaff would talk, when
he lay picking the bed-clothes, and smiling on his fingers' ends ;
and he knew exactly what part of his babbling talk would be
remembered and repeated by Mrs. Quickly.   Moreover, he
had faith in Shakespeare, and believed that he would reproduce
all this ; and he had moreover the necessary knowledge of
Elizabethan orthography, such as this, that *babbled* was ordi-
narily spelt *babled*.   Thus was he led to an emendation which
has covered Shakespeare with glory and been identified with his
text.   (See *Notes and Queries*, 1st S. viii. 314, for an eloquent
commentary on this scene, written in the vein of Dr. John
Brown ; and also *The Grammar of Assent*, pp. 264 — 270,
where Dr. Newman takes the corrupt passage of the folio, with
its various emendations, as the concrete example of complex
inference.)

No amount of sagacity or ingenuity in the critic can com-
pensate the want of appropriate learning and scholarship.   In
some instances, indeed, if he have sagacity to catch the hidden
sense of a corrupt passage, and ingenuity in conjecture, a great
step may be made towards its restoration.   But success in any
case presupposes the appropriate knowledge.   Dr. E. A. Abbott's
elaborate but still imperfect *Shakespearian Grammar* will at

* He must have been reading Brewster's *Optics*, 1831, p. 296, where
the author proposes an observation, on 'a pen lying upon a green cloth.'

least serve to testify to the fact that the grammar of Shakespeare and his contemporaries is not at all that of our written tongue, and Dyce's *Glossary*, and Dr. Alexander Schmidt's *Shakespeare-Lexicon*, will afford abundant evidence of the fact that there was a treasury of words open to an Elizabethan writer, which are now obsolete, or else current in senses more or less different from those which the words imported in the fourteenth and fifteenth centuries.

For other aids to conjecture in the vindication or the restoration of the text, one of the most valuable is the collation of passages more or less parallel, occurring in Shakespeare's plays and poems. For example : in *All's Well that Ends Well*, ii. 3, is an equivocal construction which has misled many an editor. Lafeu says,

> They say miracles are past, and we have our Philosophicall persons, to make moderne and familiar things supernaturall and causelesse. (Fo. 1623.)

Some editors insert a comma after ' things,' so as to force the construction into discord with what follows :

> Hence is it, that we make trifles of terrours, ensconcing our selves into seeming knowledge, when we should submit our selves to an unknowne feare.

This ought to settle the matter for every one : but if any doubt should linger over the phrase 'to make modern and familiar, things supernatural and causeless,' the following parallel would remove it :

> Thou dost make possible, things not so held.—*Winter's Tale*, i. 2.

As here things not held possible are made so, so in the former passage, things supernatural and causeless are made modern and familiar. To take a far more difficult passage; in *Timon of Athens*, iii. 3, Sempronius exclaims,

> How ? Have they deny'de him ?
> Has Ventidgius and Lucullus deny'de him,
> And does he send to me ? Three ? Humh ?
> It showes but little love, or judgment in him.
> Must I be his last Refuge ? His Friends (like Physitians)
> Thrive, give him over : Must I take th' Cure upon me ?

The mention of Lucius, Lucullus, and Ventidius (explaining the ejaculation 'Three') has been thought to favour Johnson's conjecture, that 'thrive' is a misprint for *thrice:* q. d. these three friends have one after another given him over, just as physicians give over their patient. But a parallel passage in the fourth act of the same play, seems to us quite sufficient to justify the text as it stands in the folio. Timon addressing the banditti, says,

> Trust not the physitian,
> His Antidotes are poyson, and he slayes
> More then you Rob : Take wealth and lives together, &c.

i. e., he advises the robbers to take the physicians as their examples, who thrive by their patients' wealth first, and leave them to die of their drugs afterwards. We maintain, then, that in the former place Sempronius is intended to say, that Timon's friends act by him as physicians do by their patients, *thrive* by him, and then *give him over*. Till the singular force of this parallel can be explained away, it is an impertinence to treat the suspected passage as corrupt.

Another case, where a passage ought to help us to restore an undoubtedly corrupt text, is in *Measure for Measure*, ii. 1, Escalus says,

> Well, heaven forgive him; and forgive us all:
> *Some rise by sinne, and some by vertue fall:*
> Some run from brakes of Ice, and answer none,
> And some condemned for a fault alone.

The second line being in italics in the folio 1623, we may safely regard these three lines as the vestiges of an older play, or as an interpolation by an inferior hand: but certainly they must have had sense once; while at present the line following that in italics is quite innocent of meaning. Apparently 'and answer none' means, *and are not called to account;* since in the last line we are told that judgment is passed on others for a single fault—a mere fault. Accordingly one would expect to find the corrupt line signifying, that *some run through a course of increasing wickedness, without being called to account.* Now there is a passage in *Cymbeline*, v. 1, which is of good service to us at this pinch. Posthumus says, addressing the Gods,

> But alacke,
> You snatch some hence for little faults; that's love
> To have them fall no more: you some permit
> To second illes with illes, each elder worse, &c.

We have here the same counter-assertions, but in the reverse order: reading them thus,

U

> You some permit
> To second illes with illes, each elder worse,
> You snatch some hence for little faults ;

and comparing this with the passage from *Measure for Measure*, we can hardly help believing that the line

> Some run from brakes of Ice, and answer none,

ought to assert, that some run through a long career of sin going on ever from bad to worse, without being called to account. Without some further *datum* it is hardly possible to propose a satisfactory emendation of the passage. 'Ice' can hardly be an error for *Vice*, as Rowe suggested ; for it is from the 'brakes,' or restraints, of virtue (of just*ice*, in fact) that the delinquents run. It has occurred to us that the text, as it stands, may admit of an unstrained interpretation, which, however, would fix upon the suspected line a very awkward and unusual metaphor. We have observed that Chapman affords several examples of *brake*, used in a peculiar sense :

> Or (like a strumpet) learne to set my lookes
> In an eternall *Brake*, or practise juggling,
> To keepe my face still fast, my hart still loose;
>
> *Bussy D'Ambois*, i. 1.

Evidently, these two phrases are equivalent :

> To set my looks in an eternal brake

is just

> to keep my face still fast :

and omitting 'eternal' from the one, and 'still' from the other, it follows that to set anything in a *brake* is to keep it fast and fixed. The word, indeed, was technically used for a horse's bit. But the phrase 'to set *my looks* in an eternal brake' means something more than restraint: *brake* is here a *fixed form.* We have the word again, in *Byron's Tragedie*, iv. 1. We must quote the dialogue to understand the metaphor:

D'Auvergne.	See, see, not one of them will cast a glaunce
	At our eclipsed faces;
Byron.	they keepe all
	To cast in admiration on the King :
	For *from his face are all their faces moulded.*
D'Au.	But when a change comes ; we shall see them all
	Chang'd into water, that will instantly
	Give looke for looke, &c.
Byr.	Is't not an easie losse to lose theyr lookes,
	Whose hearts so soone are *melted* ?
	* * * * *
	See in how grave a *Brake* he sets his vizard: [*i. e.,* visage]
	Passion of nothing ; &c.

Here we have the people's faces set in *brakes*, which, as soon as their hearts are *melted*, thaw too, and *change into water.* What are these but ' brakes of Ice ' ? What do such faces, but ' run from brakes of ice,' and turn to water which can take any shape ? Now Shakespeare, as we would read him, in the *crux* in *Measure for Measure,* is asserting *(voce Eschyli)* that some, whose *characters* are set in brakes of ice, *i. e.,* with no shew of passion whatever, do run from them, under the heat of lust, and are not called to account ('answer none') while others are condemned for a single fault.* Be this as it may, it

---

* Cleopatra (*Antony and Cleopatra*, v. 2) had set herself in an ice-brake, from which she would never more run, when she exclaimed :

> My resolution's plact, and I have nothing
> Of woman in me : now from head to foot
> I'm marble constant ; &c.

is remarkable that the passage in *Cymbeline* should afford an exact analogue to the line which in the folio is printed in italics,

Some rise by sin, and some by virtue fall.

The line following 'each elder worse' is probably corrupt, viz.,

To make them dread it, to the doer's thrift;

but we know well enough what it ought to *mean*, though we have not yet discovered what it ought to *say:* it should mean, that the Gods allow the sinner to run his course, that, in the event, like the prodigal son, his stomach may rise against the husks and wash, and that he may voluntarily return to a cleanly life. Such *rise by sin*, while those who *fall by virtue* are snatched away that they may fall no more. It is, we think, quite probable that by the aid of this analogy the line, if corrupt, may be some day restored. At present it must remain a case of doubtful interpretation or of inchoate restoration, like the *sorrow-wagge* and *busie-lest* passages, which demands patient consideration, not immediate decision.

Here, however, is one from *Coriolanus*, ii. 1, which contains two probable corruptions, the former admits of an easy and seemingly a conclusive remedy. Let us premise that 'him' here means Marcius, not the baby.

Your prattling Nurse
Into a rapture lets her Baby crie,
While she chats him.

'Chats him' is, we think, corrupt; and many conjectures have been made, all alike inadmissible. Perhaps '*claps* him'

is the best, but the metre halts for it. As to the other place,
Mr. Justice Blackstone (*Shakespeare Society's Papers*, i. 99)
remarks, 'A RAPTURE is an odd effect of crying in Babies.
Dr. * * * would read it RUPTURE. Only Qu. If crying
ever produces *this* Effect?' To which he adds, 'I have since
enquired, and am told that it is usual.' Probably most fathers
and mothers know that such is the fact. But Blackstone
might have learned it from a sixteenth century work, viz.,
Phioravante's Secrets, 1582, p. 5, where we read,

'To helpe yong Children of the Rupture.

The Rupture is caused two waies, the one through weaknesse
of the place, and the other through much criyng.'

This emendation was independently proposed by two other
critics (see the Cambridge Edition of *Shakespeare*, vi. 316);
and it seems as good as an emendation can be; yet it has never
been adopted, because it was conceived that the word in the
text admitted of explanation and defense. Certainly 'rapture'
is just *seizure:* cf. Chapman's *Iliad*, xxii. (Taylor's ed. ii.;
192); and *Pericles*, ii. 1, where 'rupture' is, as was pointed out
by Dr. Sewell, an error of the press for *rapture:*

> And spite of all the rupture of the sea,
> This jewel holds his biding on my arm.

Mr. J. P. Collier (*Farther Particulars*, 1839, p. 41) quotes
the parallel passage from the novel on which Shakespeare's
play was founded : the hero says he got to land 'with a jewell
whom all the *raptures* of the sea could not bereave from
his arme.' But there seems no sufficient authority for the

employment of *rapture* in the sense of *fit* or *convulsion:* and that
being so, we adhere to Blackstone's emendation, and believe
that just as *rapture* in *Pericles* was misprinted *rupture,* so
rupture in *Coriolanus* was misprinted *rapture.* At the same
time we must bear in mind that Steevens adduced, in support
of the old text, the following quotation, which at least must
'give us pause':

> 'Your darling will weep itself into a rapture, if you do not
> take heed.'—*The Hospitall for London Follies,* 1602.

We conclude this essay with a restoration which is not due
to conjectural ingenuity, but to the contemporary authority of
Ben Jonson. According to him, Shakespeare, in his *Julius
Cæsar,* iii. 1, wrote as follows:

> *Cæsar.* Thy brother by decree is banished :
>   If thou dost bend and pray and fawn for him,
>   I spurn thee like a cur out of my way.
> *Metellus.* Cæsar, thou dost me wrong,
> *Cæsar.* Cæsar did never wrong but with just cause,
>   Nor without cause will he be satisfied.
> *Metellus.* Is there no voice more worthy than my own, &c. ;

and somewhater later (iii. 2) we read,

> *Second Citizen.* If thou consider rightly of the matter,
>   Cæsar has had great wrong.
> *Third Citizen.* Has he, master?

But the folio, our only authority for *Julius Cæsar,* does not
give Metellus' remark, but continues Cæsar's address thus,

> Know, Cæsar doth not wrong, nor without cause
> Will he be satisfied.

Now this is *à propos* of nothing. There is nothing in Cæsar's speech preceding these two lines to lead to the denial, 'Cæsar doth not wrong' (for Metellus does not provoke it); and besides, the second line is unfinished.

To Ben Jonson's *Timber or Discoveries; made upon men and matter:* &c. (Works, 1640-1, fol., vol. ii., p. 97), we are indebted for the preservation of the original text in iii. 1, as we have given it. But the editors, deeming its adoption an act of un-faithfulness to the folio, will not have it. Mr. Halliwell indeed says (*Life of Shakespeare*, 1848, p. 185), 'Take Jonson's words as literally true, and the whole becomes clear,' &c.; and he has a like note on the text, in his magnificent Folio Edition of Shakespeare: but he had not the courage to act on his con-viction, and regulate the text on Jonson's authority. Pope had the temerity to propose substituting for the reply of the Third Citizen, in iii. 2, the altered line,

> Cæsar had never wrong, but with just cause,

thus making the plebeian a sympathiser with Brutus. The text in iii. 1, as we have first given it, was charged upon Shakespeare as a bull; but Ben Jonson does not tell us that Shakespeare changed it in consequence; nor have we any reason for believing that he would have cared for the laughter of his censors. *Nostro judicio* Ben's critique is captious. The justice of the cause is not inconsistent with wrong. Mr. Halliwell rightly observes, 'If *wrong* is taken in the sense of *injury** or *harm*,

---

* *Injury*, here, is an instance of the same ambiguity.

as Shakespeare sometimes uses it, there is no absurdity in the line, " He shall have wrong," 2 *Henry VI.,* v. 1.' (*Life of Shakespeare,* 1848, p. 185.)   Again, in *A Winter's Tale,* v. 1, Paulina, speaking of the hapless Queen, says,

> Had she such power,
> She had just cause.
>
> *Leontes.*   She had, and would incense me
> To murther her I married.

(*i. e.,* her whom he might take as his second wife).   Clearly, then, the Queen has, in Leontes' judgment, *just cause* to incense him to do another a grievous wrong.   This is even more amenable to Jonson's censure than the line which fell under it.   The Cambridge editors most absurdly charge Jonson with a lapse of memory; and this, too, in the face of the additional facts, that the folio reading is defective both in sense and in measure, and that Jonson reverts to the same censure in the *Induction* to his *Staple of News.*

Where then was the blunder?   We say it was Jonson's, and his fellow censors': that the line they laughed at was and is unimpeachable good sense, and that it is the editor's duty to use Jonson's censure for the purpose of correcting the folio reading, and restoring the passage to that form in which, as we believe, it flowed from the pen of Shakespeare.

With anything but pleasing auguries we bring this somewhat desultory essay to a close.   Though wishing to treat our opponents with all the ceremony prescribed by the law of arms, we have not been loath to strike in earnest, in support and vindication of a literary heritage which is, in our eyes, far too precious to be made the sport of every ingenious guesser, whose vanity impels him to turn critic or editor. There are early dramatic works enough for such men to try their 'prentice-hands upon, without intruding into that paradise 'where angels fear to tread.' For the fashion of this day in dealing with the text of Shakespeare we have no kind of respect, scarcely any tolerance. We have yet to learn what right a combination of dulness, ignorance, arrogance, and bad taste has to respectful usage; and of such stuff are most of the later critics on Shakespeare made, with a few honourable exceptions. Of the bulk of their criticism we have taken no kind of note in the foregoing discussions. In a few select cases we have endeavoured, with such knowledge and ability as we possess, to show how superior is the old text to the readings by which it has been proposed to supersede it; and where we may have failed in the performance of our task, we have sufficient faith in that text to charge ourselves with the whole blame of the failure.

Reluctant as we are to subject any part of the old text to the crucible of conjecture, we have given ample justification of its use, and indicated the limits within which this kind of criticism may be fruitful; but on this subject the ablest critics may differ, and on the issues involved we cannot always anticipate as the reward of study those final decisions which will assuredly be conferred by time.

X

Supplementary Notes.

—o—

ON reviewing the foregoing chapters we find a few points on which something we have said calls for correction, explanation, or addition. Had these notes occurred to us in time, some would have been incorporated with the text, and some would have been appended as foot-notes.

P. 17. Chapman too has *swownings* in *The Widdowe's Teares*, v. 1.

P. 33. Possibly *land-damn* may not long remain unreduced. In *Notes and Queries*, 5th S., iii. 464, the following explanation is given of the word:

> Forty years ago an old custom was still in use in this district [*i. e.*, Buxton]. When any slanderer was detected, or any parties discovered in adultery, it was usual to *lan-dan* them. This was done by the rustics traversing from house to house along the 'country side,' blowing trumpets and beating drums or pans and kettles. When an audience was assembled, the delinquents' names were proclaimed, and they were thus *land-damned*.

This is plausible; but Mr. Hensleigh Wedgwood, in *Notes and Queries*, 5th S., iv. 3, points out that *landan*, like *randan*, is 'a mere representation of continued noise.' Land-damning might mean the 'drier death ashore' mentioned by Proteus in *The Two Gentlemen of Verona*, i. 1, and referred to with infinite humour by Gonzalo in *The Tempest*, i. 1. All other interpretations may, we think, be firmly put aside.

P. 35. In contending that Shakespeare's *cyme* means what we call *Brussels sprouts*, Mr. H. A. J. Munro identifies it, *not* with Holland's *cyme* (singular), but with Pliny's *cymae* (plural): *i. e.*, he accents the 'e.'

P. 44. There is yet another instance in Shakespeare of the 'relative absolute,' viz., in *King John*, ii. 2.

> maids,
> Who having no external thing to lose
> But the word maid, [he] cheats the poor maid of that ; &c.

P. 61. Another instance of the expression *points of war*, occurs in the Preface to *Sadducismus Triumphatus*, by the Rev. Joseph Glanvil:

> For an hour together it would beat ' Round-Heads and Cuckolds,' the
> ' Tattoo,' and several other *points of war*, as well as any drummer.

P. 67. ' Hold and *occupie* a rocke :' cf.,

> *Judges*, xvi, 11. If they bind me fast with new ropes that never were
> *occupied*, then I shall be weak, and be as another man.

St. Jerome bade Paula *hold and make use of a distaff.*

P. 72. We have followed Steevens' quotation: but in the edition reprinted by Mr. J. P. Collier in 1844, and by Mr. Charles Hindley in 1871, the title is differently spelt, and Jalowsy says,

> She that is fayre, lusty and yonge
> And can comon in termes wyth fyled tonge
> And wyll *abyde* whysperynge in the eare
> *Thynke* ye her tayle is not *lyght* of the seare.

P. 78 (note). ' The Palais de Luxembourg ' is, we are afraid, a slip for the Hôtel Cluny. Doubtless many of our readers will remember the ivory-fetter preserved there (Silvio's was of gold) ; and also the effigy of a lady over one of the doorways in the Castle of Heidelberg.

P. 80, § 8. We should have included in this class that well-known *crux* in *The Winter's Tale*, iii. 2

> I ne'er heard yet
> That any of these bolder vices wanted
> Less impudence to gainsay what they did
> Than to perform it first.

The central notion once seized, we are led to take ' less ' as an adjective qualifying ' impudence,' not as an adverb qualifying ' wanted,' as Johnson and others have mistaken it. Having in.. udence enough to perform those vices, the depraved would not be likely to want the less impudence necessary to repudiate them and to deny their performance. A parallel case in *Antony and Cleopatra*, iv. 12, is familiar to all students of the text.

P. 81. After this was printed we witnessed at the Brentwood dog-show (July 13, 1875), the most perfect exemplification of the ridicule which is provoked by the secondary awkwardness of dissimulation. A visitor, who was evidently no scholar, was endeavouring to decipher the warning over the first dog in the show—a huge mastiff of the Lyme breed. He had got as far as DAN when, approaching the stand to get a better view of the word, the dog instantly seized him by the arm. This gentleman evidently thought that indifference was the wiser part of valour; for, even while he turned white with fear, he ejaculated—'Oh! I don't mind it at all: I'm used to the bite of dogs.'

P. 85. Just as we required a basis for the pun on 'wax,' so we do for that on 'laughter' in *The Tempest*, ii. 1.

> *Sebastian.* Done: The wager?
> *Antonio.* A laughter.
> *Sebastian.* A match.

Laughter may be the cant name for some small coin (a doit or a denier) commonly *laid* in betting. At present the only meaning of the word (*laughter, lafter, lawter*) is a setting of eggs laid at one time. The word is in Brockett, and is still in provincial use: a gamekeeper at Yoxford, Suffolk, told us that he found he had better luck with the second *lawter* (of pheasants' eggs) than with the first.

'Laughter' in *Julius Cæsar* ('I am no common laughter') is just a *broker*, in the bad sense: but its history is at present shrouded in obscurity.

P. 86. *A propos* of this soliloquy we may add, to obviate a misconception which we know to exist, that the line

> There's the respect
> That makes calamity of so long life:

means just this:

> There [we see] the reason why we put up with calamity so long,
> [instead of ending it by suicide].

This is a good instance of the virtue of paraphrase, *pace* Mr. Meiklejohn.

P. 87. We might have quoted from *King John*, ii. 2,

> John   *   *   *   hath willingly *departed* with a part.

and from *Love's Labour's Lost*, ii. 1,

> Which we much rather had *depart* withal.

and from *Every Woman in her Humour*, 1609 (a passage quoted by Steevens),

> She'll serve under him till death us depart.

also from the *Comedy of Errors*, iii. 1:

> In debating which was best, we shall *part* with neither,

'where,' says Monk Mason, '*part* means to depart, to go away.'

P. 94. On the varying prosody of such words see Shepherd's *History of the English Language* (New York, Hale and Son), p. 170.

P. 97. A curious illustration of the lines

> And blowne with restlesse violence round about
> The pendant world

occurs at the end of Cicero's *Vision of Scipio*, thus rendered by Mr. C. E. Edmonds:

> For the soules of those men who are devoted to corporeal pleasures, and who having yielded themselves as it were as servants to them, enslaved to pleasures under the impulse of their passions, have violated the laws of Gods and men ; such soul's, having escaped from their bodies, *hover round the earth*, nor do they return to this place, *till they have been tossed about for many ages.*

P. 117. To this list might, we think, be added the following:

> Or I shall shew the cynders of my spirits
> Through th' Ashes of my chance.—*Antony and Cleopatra*, v. 2.
> Through the Ashes of my *glance.*—(Ingleby.)

This, like most good emendations, requires support and illustration. First: ' the ashes of my chance' is nonsense. Hanmer's mischance (for 'my chance') is no better. Warburton's *my cheeks* was a weak conjecture, which he never adopted. Sidney Walker's *change* is unsatisfactory. Secondly: note that Cleopatra has just said,

> What goest thou back? thou shalt
> Go backe I warrant thee: but *Ile catch thine eyes*
> *Though they had wings.*

She would burn him up with her glance—what Milton calls 'the charm of Beauty's powerful glance' (*Paradise Lost*, viii. 533)—and though the fire had almost faded out, the very cinders would smite him. Thirdly: for illustration let us recur once more to Mrs. Beecher Stowe, who thus describes Cassy's glance, in *Uncle Tom's Cabin*, 1853 (Routledge), p. 382.

> A glance like sheet-lightning suddenly flashed from those black eyes; and, facing about, with quivering lip and dilated nostrils, she drew herself up, and fixed a glance, blazing with rage and scorn, on the driver.

(We suppose when the 'glance' became 'fixed,' it was no longer a *glance* but a *gaze*.) Compare also the description of Cassy's feelings on p. 399:

> When Legree brought Emmeline to the house, all the *smouldering embers* of womanly feeling *flashed up* in the worn heart of Cassy, and she took part with the girl.

Cleopatra just says, she will shew the still smouldering embers of her spirits through the ashes of her faded glance, just as we see the hot gleads through the ashes of an expiring fire.

P. 120. In a proof of this very Essay, we observe a parallel misprint, viz., 'there formation of character,' for 'the reformation of character,' &c.

P. 140. Was Hamlet reading St. Augustine? Be that as it may, the following passage is a curious illustration of Hamlet's simile between the operation of the sun in breeding maggots in carrion, and that of a king (*e. g.*, Cophetua) in loving a beggar maid, or himself in wooing the chancellor's daughter. I am indebted to Mr. C. J. Monro for this illustration: it is from St. Augustine, *De fide et symbolo*, § 10. (Vol. xi, p. 512, of the 3rd Venetian edition [1797] of the Benedictine labours.)

> Nec nobis fidem istam minuat cogitatio muliebrium viscerum, ut propterea recusanda videatur talis Domini nostri generatio, quod eam sordidi sordidam putant. Quia et stultum Dei sapientius esse hominibus, et omnia munda mundis, verissime apostolus dicit. Debent igitur intueri qui hoc putant, solis huius radios, quem certe non tanquam creaturam Dei laudant sed *tanquam Deum adorant*, per cloacarum foetores et

quaecumque horribilia usquequaque diffundi et *in his operari secundum naturam suam*, nec tamen inde aliqua contaminantione sordescere, cum visibilis lux visibilibus sordibus sit natura coniunctior ; quanto minus igitur poterat pollui Verbum Dei non corporeum neque visibile de femineo corpore ubi humanam carnem suscepit cum anima et spiritu, quibus intervenientibus habitat maiestas Verbi ab humani corporis fragilitate secretius.

If Shakespeare had St. Augustine in mind when he wrote this scene, what English book did he use ?

PASSAGES IN SHAKESPEARE

DISCUSSED IN

THE STILL LION.

—*0*—

Y

Hee that a Foole doth very wisely hit,
Doth very foolishly, although he smart
Seeme senselesse of the bob.   If not,
The Wise-man's folly is anathomiz'd
Even by the squandering glances of the foole.   -   -   *Ibid.*, ii. 6   81

One inch of delay more, is a South-sea of discoverie. -   *Ibid.*, iii. 2   80

       Who might be your mother,
That you insult, exult, and all at once,
Over the wretched? -   -   -   -   -   -   *Ibid.*, iii. 5   79

Turning your Bookes to Graves, your Inke to Blood,
Your Pennes to Launces, and your Tongue divine
To a lowd Trumpet, and a Point of Warre.   2 *Henry VI*, iv. 1   60

Ye shall have hempen caudle then, and the helpe of hatchet.
                        Ibid., iv. 7   29
And yet the spacious bredth of this division
Admits no Orifex for a point as subtle
As *Ariachne's* broken woofe to enter :   *Troilus and Cressida*, v. 2   64

I do beseech thee, remember thy courtesy; I beseech thee, apparel
    thy head.   -   -   -   -   -   *Love's Labour's Lost*, v. 1   74

I will bring thee where Mistris *Anne Page* is, at a Farm-house a
    Feasting: and thou shalt wooe her: Cride-game, said I well?
                The Merry Wives of Windsor, ii. 3   75

            my free drift
Halts not particularly, but moves itself
In a wide sea of wax: &c.   -   -   -   *Timon of Athens*, i. 1   83

        How?   Have they deny'de him?
Has Ventidgius and Lucullus deny'de him,
And does he send to me?   Three?   Humh?
It showes but little love, or judgment in him.
Must I be his last Refuge?   His Friends (like Physitians)
Thrive, give him over: Must I take th' Cure upon me?
                      Ibid., iii. 3   144

PAGE

Now the Gods keepe you old enough,
That you may live
Onely in bone, that none may looke on you. -   -   *Ibid.*, iii. 5   135

        we must all part
Into this sea of air.   -   -   -   -   -   -   *Ibid.*, iv. 2   87

Thought I thy spirits were stronger than thy shames,
Myself would on the rearward of reproaches
Strike at thy life.   -   -   *Much Ado About Nothing*, iv. 1   93

Bring me a father that so lov'd his childe,
Whose joy of her is overwhelm'd like mine,
And bid him speake of patience.
If such a one will smile and stroke his beard,
And sorrowe, wagge, crie hem, when he should grone, &c.
                Ibid., v. 1   129

I love thee not a jar o' the clock behind
What lady she her lord.   -   -   -   *The Winter's Tale*, i. 2   116

        If it prove
Shee's otherwise, Ile keep my Stables where
I lodge my Wife, Ile goe in couples with her:
Then when I feele, and see her, no farther trust her.   *Ibid.*, ii. 1   76

        I ne'er heard yet
That any of these bolder vices wanted
Less impudence to gainsay what they did
Than to perform it first.   -   -   -   -   -   *Ibid.*, iii. 2   157

        no: this my Hand will rather
The multitudinous Seas incarnadine,
Making the Greene one, Red.   -   -   -   -   *Macbeth*, ii. 2   119

Her Gentlewomen, like the Nereides,
So many Mer-maides tended her i' th' eyes,
And made their bends adornings.   At the Helme
A seeming Mer-maide steers.   *Antony and Cleopatra*, ii. 2   119

        The mean time, lady,
I'll raise the preparation of a war
Shall stain your brother   -   -   -   -   -   *Ibid.*, iii. 4   96

AUTHORS QUOTED.

— 0 —

CORRECTION.

P. 61, l. 12. *For* In *read* It.